Total Joy

By Marabel Morgan

The Total Woman
Total Joy

Marabel Morgan

Total Joy

FLEMING H. REVELL COMPANY
Old Tappan, New Jersey

Unless otherwise identified, Scripture references in this volume are from The Living Bible, Copyright © 1971 by Tyndale House Publishers, Wheaton, Illinois 60187. All rights reserved.

Scripture quotations identified KJV are from the King James Version of the Bible.

Illustrations in *Total Joy* are by Russell Willeman.

To write to Marabel Morgan, or for information concerning Total Woman classes, address Total Woman, P.O. Box 380277, Miami, Fla. 33138

Library of Congress Cataloging in Publication Data

Morgan, Marabel.
    Total joy.

    Bibliography: p.
    1. Marriage—Conduct of life. 3. Women—
Psychology. I. Title.
HQ734.M826   301.42'7   76-45830
ISBN 0-8007-0816-4

To my husband, Charlie, my best friend and roommate,
and
To my daughters
Laura and Michelle,
the delights of my life

Contents

PART THREE
THE JOY OF LOVING

Acknowledgments

To my newfound friends,
    those special people
    who have shared with me their
        inspiration,
        encouragement,
        sorrows, and
        joys—
thank you.

I hope your stories will be as
    meaningful to others as they
    have been to me.

Introduction

"My name is Marabel Morgan," I said without emotion to the TV panel of "To Tell the Truth." Two other women also claimed to be Marabel Morgan, one of them a six-foot-tall single girl who told me privately she would *never* marry.

As the panelists queried the three Marabels, Soupy Sales asked, "Is there life after marriage?"

Love Story

Twelve years ago, when Charlie and I were dating, life was so beautiful. My heart just sang as I thought ahead to our wedding day. I could hardly wait. Not just for life after marriage, but for the coziest home and most intimate relationship ever.

Ten years ago, my moonlight and roses had turned to daylight and dishes. As Mrs. Morgan, I had settled into my newfound role and taken on a project: change Charlie. Nothing major—just a few minor points. The marriage "blahs" had already settled in. We were polite, of course, but there was little romance. The zip had turned to zap in two short years.

Seven years ago, Charlie and I weren't romantic, or polite, or hardly even talking to each other. My quest for marriage survival began in earnest—my project: change Marabel.

Six years ago, Charlie and I began to be more in love than even before we were married. I tried different ideas to revive romance. As a result, right before my very eyes, Charlie began to "come alive." Even my little girls, Laura and Michelle, noticed the difference. In my excitement I shared my ideas with one special girl friend, then other friends, then classes. I wrote my story in *The Total Woman* to help others avoid my mistakes, and to give ideas for success in marriage.

Since that time I would like to say that Charlie has become the Total Man, and that I have become the Total Woman, and that everything has been just super great every day.

But I can't.

He hasn't. I haven't. It hasn't.

Life, each day, is a struggle.

Problems and Praise

An incredible number of letters from all over America and many countries throughout the world have poured into my mailbox telling how creative women everywhere have applied the principles of *The Total Woman* in their own houses.

Wading through this paper avalanche, I have come to the conclusion that women and men have certain basic needs, regardless of who they are, where they live, or what they do.

I have laughed with a newlywed in Texas, cried with a divorcee in New York, and prayed with a mother in London. By sharing through correspondence, I have come to know and love so many new friends. Some of you readers may be some of those writers. If so, please read this book as a personal letter from me to you.

The letters cover every subject that I ever imagined. Most of them fall into two categories—problems and praise. The problems reveal heartache, conflict, and tragedy. The praises are exciting testimonies of changed lives and marriages. I wanted to share some of these stories with you.

Of course, I have at all times respected the privacy of the writers. Often, the irrelevant facts have been changed, not that the actual names and places really matter anyway. Rather, I hope the particular problems and responses will be as helpful to you as they have been to me.

These events are a glimpse inside 395 Main Street,

Anywhere, USA. Looking in, you may meet your neighbor or your mother-in-law, or some warm and wonderful new friends. Who knows—you may even spot yourself in the mirror.

If you haven't read *The Total Woman,* don't worry. We'll start off together from here. First, the bad news— the problem letters. The following excerpts from letters read like classified ads:

HELP WANTED!

I need help! I've only been married six months and my husband and I do not talk or make love. Please help!

I've been married 35 years. Something's been missing for about 30. He and I have not kissed in years. Interaction is on a hate level, although I really love him.

I have just finished reading your book. You sound like a total nut to me! But with a twenty-year-old marriage that is a total failure, who am I to judge? Quick! Somebody! Anybody! Everybody! Help!

My husband and I have been divorced for five months. I was a moody, sloppy, nagging wife.

He has found someone else to take my place. Naturally, I can't blame him. I realize now I pushed him out the door.

I've been married (second time) one year and it's going to pieces fast. I'm desperate. I can't seem to unlearn all those bad habits. I know I'm driving him off. I am 45. We are not kids. Please help!

I need help for my life's sake. I'm backed up against a wall with very little crawl space left. I've never considered suicide but I'm looking for purpose and meaning. I have a beautiful family and a husband that's tops. It's me I'm worried about. I'm messing up what I have and don't know how to stop.

My husband is a minister, and we are at the point of divorce. Who can we talk to?

We have been married 42 years and I can't get any cooperation from my wife. Please send me all information you can. Am I too old at 76 to dream of a Total Woman?

I am not a psychiatrist or a marriage counselor or a lawyer, and I certainly don't claim that *The Total Woman* principles will solve every woman's every problem. So many needs are quite severe and may require professional help, either medically, emotionally, or spiritually.

But unfortunately in many cases the ones with the most desperate problems either do not or cannot receive the help they need, so they just limp along through life operating at 25 percent efficiency. In the process they affect husbands, children, friends, and everyone else they meet.

Hundreds of women have lamented a lack of marriage know-how as part of their problem. One woman admitted she just didn't know how to bring happiness to herself or her husband. "There must be an answer," she wrote. "I know that divorce won't solve anything, but I can't cope. It's a shame that we aren't prepared for raising a family in a happy home. At least, I wasn't."

I wasn't either. While growing up, I never saw a happy marriage. Maybe that's why it's so thrilling to find a plan of action that works.

Salvage Value

Charlie and I talked recently with a couple who were calling their marriage quits. After we listened a while, I felt frustrated. Strangely, neither the man nor his wife could give any real reason for the divorce. They had no outside lovers. They didn't fight. In fact, they both said, "We are the best of friends!"

Bewildered, Charlie and I discussed their situation with a psychiatrist, whose practice mostly involved marital counseling. He said that in many of those cases, the problem was not an emotional disturbance at all, but rather a matter of the will. "If neither party wants the marriage to continue," he told us, "all the courts, lawyers, and psychiatrists in the world can't keep them together."

I remember how I felt when our marriage was in trouble. Instead of a divorce, I wanted a better marriage, so I embarked on a course of action designed to keep it alive and make it zing! My marriage was more important to me than the few silly things which were causing our arguments.

This book, therefore, is based on the premise that a woman wants her marriage—if she has one—to succeed. If she isn't interested in saving it, this book is not for her. Her starting premises are exactly opposite from mine; our conclusions will be worlds apart!

On the other hand, you may want your marriage to survive and sizzle, but you don't think there's a prayer. If so, please stay on the bus a little longer. I have seen so many remarkable turnarounds that I would encourage you to make one more try. A recent NBC-TV documentary in New York on *The Total Woman* program was entitled "How to Succeed at Marriage by Really Trying." I believe that's the key—*by really trying.*

If you are single, I hope you will still find many of these suggestions and examples helpful. Most of the principles in this book (except for a few portions, such as sex) apply in all human relationships: with your boss, your dates, your mailman, and your sister-in-law. You probably already know most or all of these principles anyway. After all, there is really nothing new under the sun, but we all need to be reminded from time to time. Since I am married, naturally I'm concerned about marriage relationships, and I need lots of reminders.

Is there life after marriage?

There can be. Marriage need not be a drag, but before a woman can help revive her husband or children, I believe she must first find her own identity and release her own personality. Only then can marriage be exciting and fun. Only then can she have a true zest for life and be able to change the mundane into an adventure.

Part One
The Joy of Being

1 Who Am I?

When I was in the third grade, my mother and father were in the throes of divorce. All day long at school my thoughts dwelled on the upheaval at home. I was being wrenched between one parent and the other. All during my elementary years, I felt empty and devastated. Life seemed so uncertain.

After six years the divorce was still unresolved. I had packed and unpacked my few belongings at least a dozen times. My dad always watched me while I packed. He controlled his tears but I couldn't control mine.

I lost all the confidence I ever had. Going to school each day was such agony. Sometimes I felt so out of step I simply babbled if anyone looked my way. I felt terribly embarrassed about being me.

One humiliating experience threw me over the edge.

In an eighth-grade history class, the teacher called on me to stand and read a passage. As I stood up, I felt incredibly inferior. Those feelings of inadequacy swept over me, strangling my words. My heart pounded with fear. The classroom began to whirl as I tried to read aloud, and I fainted dead away in the aisle.

Later that day I was aware of my classmates laughing and talking about me. Fear gripped me after that—fear of others' evaluation of me. Fear of feeling totally rejected.

Today, when I read letters from women who are asking themselves, "Who am I?" I know their turmoil, their heartache, and their paralyzing fear.

Their circumstances, of course, are different from mine—sometimes far worse than anything I have experienced. But whether difficult or seemingly easy, I know how they feel. I identify. I've been there.

In December of my ninth-grade year, my father died. Part of me died too. My sorrow overwhelmed me. School overwhelmed me. I ate lunch each day alone. With my confidence at zero, I crawled into a shell to escape. I consciously began to wonder what life was all about and whether it was worth it.

One cold, winter day, I remember riding home on a city bus. The memory is still vivid. It was three o'clock in the afternoon. I was fourteen years old and felt eighty. Looking at the streets and trees and houses and realizing the scene was multiplied a million times around the earth sent a bittersweet ache into my heart. The world was so lovely, but I didn't know where or how I fitted in.

Sitting on that old jostling bus, I asked myself for the first time, "Who am I? Why am I here? Where am I going?"

Plain Jane

Other women have asked the same searching questions. Jane, a surburban wife, admitted to me she didn't know who she was either. Although she is attractive, she said she felt completely inadequate.

Looking in on Jane at a social gathering, you would never dream she felt lost. Why, she's the life of the party. A closer look reveals that she only acts within the rigid rules of the group. Though unspoken, these rules dictate how Jane should dress and gesture and speak. Her hairstyle is identical to the self-proclaimed leader of her group. In fact, Jane is a carbon copy of her leader. She conforms explicitly for fear the group will chew her up in little pieces at their bridge parties.

Jane did not know who she was and didn't dare to find out. She had become a slave to what "they" would think. She played the role according to the tune of her crowd. Unable to develop her own personality and talents, Jane felt only frustration as she compared herself to others. She began to hate herself. She tore down others to elevate her own self-esteem.

In a Total Woman seminar, Jane saw that she was unique. As we chatted after class, I explained, "God made you an original. Why stoop to be a copy of someone else? *You* are the most important person you can be. Don't put yourself down."

Someone once said, "Bloom where you're planted." One day Jane began to bloom and the results were dramatic. She discovered herself and had the courage to change. She became a new person.

"I had lost sight of who I was for fear of disapproval from my friends," she told me later. "I was a slave to a neurotic crew who wanted to control me. I'm not going to be a Plain Jane or Same Jane or You-Have-To Jane, anymore. I'm going to be the best *me* I can be!"

Dirty Windows

The story is told of a minister who attempted to settle a quarrel between two women in his parish. One day, he called on Marsha and listened patiently for two hours as she vented her hostility toward Betty, her neighbor. During her verbal attack she paused and stared out the window at Betty's laundry blowing on the line. "Look," she demanded full of wrath, "even her wash is dirty!" The minister looked at the sheets on the line next door and admitted to himself, they did indeed look very dirty.

Finally the pastor excused himself and went next door to visit Betty. He was immediately aware of her kind, nonjudgmental attitude, and her sorrow over having a neighbor mad at her.

During their conversation he happened to glance out her window and saw the same sheets flapping on the line. To his surprise, her wash now looked clean and white.

What had happened? Dirty sheets transformed to

clean? The minister peered out the window and then he realized. The wash looked bright because her windows were clean.

A person looking out through dirty windows sees distorted facts, feels hostility towards others, and passes the blame. Anna Russell wrote a song about this type of person who does not take personal responsibility for her own dirty windows:

> I went to my psychiatrist
>   to be psychoanalyzed,
> To find out why I killed the cat
>   and blackened my wife's eyes.
>
> He put me on a downy couch
>   to see what he could find,
> And this is what he dredged up
>   from my subconscious mind:
>
> When I was one, my mommy hid
>   my dolly in the trunk,
> And so it follows naturally,
>   that I am always drunk.
>
> When I was two, I saw my father
>   kiss the maid one day,
> And that is why I suffer now—
>   kleptomania.
>
> When I was three, I suffered from
>   ambivalence toward my brothers,
> So it follows naturally,
>   I poisoned all my lovers.

I'm so glad that I have learned
the lesson it has taught,
That everything I do that's wrong
is someone else's fault!

Homecoming Mums

If you have been passing the blame for your problems,
or merely feeling sorry for yourself like I did, how do you
crawl out of your mental rut and suddenly start to
change? By an act of your will. I finally told myself, "I'm
not going to let my past control me. I am going to change
me. I *want* to do it!" The key is in the *want to.*

All during my miserable ninth grade, I wallowed in
the mire of thinking I was destined to be alone. But by
the following September, I had had enough. Life was
passing me by. I made up my mind to lick my fears, and
the only way I knew was to meet them head-on.

To overcome my fear of speaking, I signed up for two
speech courses. I read books on public speaking, and
even entered speech contests, fighting fainting all the
way. Following through was the most frightening experience of my life, but I forced myself to do it.

The project for Homecoming that year was to sell
mums to every high-school student. I meekly volun-
teered, knowing it would bring me face-to-face with
people. Quaking with fear, I approached a student and
forced myself to run through my memorized sales pitch.
He listened and then bought a mum.

That was the beginning. With one sale came a little

confidence. I was determined to keep it up, and soon I discovered that talking to people was fun, especially when I had something to say. Some of the buyers became my friends. By the end of that week, the Student Council awarded a special prize to the person who had sold the most mums. *Me!*

The change came about because I had determined to start. My attitude began to change. I had forced myself to take action and it yielded results. From that simple project I began to develop confidence, make friends, and enjoy being me. King Solomon captured the process, "As [a man] thinketh in his heart, so is he."[1]

Grouch Times Four

My attitude at any given moment determines how I will react, regardless of my situation. My husband and kids don't *force* me to lose my temper. The pressures of life don't compel me to take pills, or drink booze, or eat my way into obesity. My problems don't cause my actions; my problems simply reveal what I am inside.

I know that my attitude usually sets the atmosphere in our house. If I'm a grouch at breakfast and sling the cereal bowls at my family, they react in the same way. Suddenly, the grouch is multiplied by four. That makes four grouches stewing at the breakfast table.

Conversely, when I attempt to set a positive atmosphere early in the morning, things seem to start so much better. Charlie and the girls also respond that way. At least, sometimes they do!

The test of my patience is not starting out in a cheery frame of mind, but rather keeping it up amid wails of broken shoestrings, lost car keys, and ripped homework.

There is no justice in being "blamed" for the sun's rising in the morning. There is no fairness in my calmly lacing up new shoestrings, sweetly producing the car keys, taping mangled homework, and sending my family happily out the door. But a certain satisfaction comes from knowing that I've done my part, and that they will feel confident out in their world.

Most mornings when I awake, I am pleasantly surprised to find I'm still alive. On occasion I have been known to wake up mean and irritable, but even then I can choose not to stay that way. Yesterday is gone and tomorrow may not come. Today is the only slot of time I really have. What a shame to blow it. I want to make today the very best possible.

Ultimate freedom, according to Dr. Viktor E. Frankl, is man's right to *choose* his own attitude in a given set of circumstances. Before I crawl out of bed, I thank the Lord for another day and ask for strength. Maybe I'm to clean the house, or work at the office, or talk with a friend over lunch. The tasks aren't the issue; my attitude is.

Sometimes I may choose to just pout or withdraw from the human race for a day, and there's a certain sadistic satisfaction in doing that too. But it doesn't compare with the exhilarating joy that comes when I fall into bed at night thinking, "What a day! I did well. I feel good. Thank You, Lord."

Potential Unlimited

Our future destination is truly out of this world. But here on earth we are designed to develop our potential, express our real selves, and in that expression, benefit each other. Each of us has unique insights and gifts that we need to share with others. The family unit is a beautiful picture of how individuals can work together to ultimately benefit mankind.

Your age, your health, and your circumstances may or may not be limitations. We are all limited in one way or another but our job is to work with our potential rather than deplore our limitations. None of us can do more than we can do.

At Disney World amusement park in Orlando, Florida, one of the mechanical dancing bears in the Country Bear Jamboree croons a line, "The guys that turn me on turn me down." I know some single girls who, like Miss Smokie, sing that same song. Since they have never accepted themselves, it's so hard for others to accept them as friends. Would-be boyfriends come around but they don't linger. They just keep movin' on.

A divorcee with three children said that since childhood she had never loved herself. She began to accept herself just as she was, starting with the scriptural origin that she was created in God's own image.[2] She later wrote to say her remarriage date had been set. "My fiance can't believe my change in attitude. He told me how my low opinion of myself had always made him feel uneasy. Now he loves the new me. I am now accomplishing what I set out to do. I have a feeling of great worth. God doesn't make junk!"

Scientists say that your human brain is composed of ten billion working parts. You are capable of accepting ten new facts every second. You have the capacity to know and understand 100 trillion different words. Talk about potential! Don't worry about your best friend's strengths. Forget what your sister-in-law has going for her. Concentrate on your potential and set your course.

Do you like what you are and what you see? If you do, that's great. But if you don't like some aspects of yourself, what are your alternatives? There are only two of which I know. Change it if you can. Accept it if you can't.

In the familiar words of Reinhold Niebuhr, "O God, give us serenity to accept what cannot be changed, the courage to change what should be changed, and wisdom to distinguish the one from the other."

The Eternal Diet

Last week my friend Becky complained to me about the weight problem that forever seems to plague her. She moaned, "I'm eternally on a diet, then a binge. Why won't I lose this weight and keep it off?"

Her question was rhetorical and she continued without a pause, "Bobby is so great. Why won't I give him what he wants—me looking tough in a bikini?"

We had just finished lunch and Becky ordered cheesecake, but was careful to use a sugar substitute in her coffee. She told me, "I lose ten pounds, then celebrate and gain it back. I know the problem is in my head."

This vicious circle is so frustrating. The worse she feels, the more she eats, and the more she eats, the worse she feels. How ironic. To escape, a woman turns to food to make herself look even worse. It's as if she is punishing the very body she hates. Looking for love and solace in food is fruitless.

"When I'm feeling blue," wrote an unhappy wife, "I eat a cookie. Better yet, I eat a bunch of cookies." In three years she had gone from a trim, attractive 95 pounds to a very unhappy 181 pounds. She thought her family didn't appreciate her, so she consoled herself by eating. "The more I ate," she said, "the more miserable I became, and now I've come to the point where I just don't care."

She probably cares but she feels helpless. I know how she feels. When I feel fat, I become depressed. Dissatisfied with myself, I try to escape. There are many escapes. Some are activities such as clubs, shopping, or sports. Some women may trip out on booze or drugs. For me, one of the easiest and least expensive escapes is drowning my sorrows in a chocolate milkshake. "One moment on the lips, but forever on the hips," as the old saying goes.

From Ohio, Jan wrote, "After reading your book, I know I'm the one who needs changing. I'm 39, weigh 288 pounds (that's right—288 pounds!). When my husband asks me to go out, I'm ashamed. Being in public is pure torture."

Whether your case is 10 pounds or 100 pounds, this

problem of weight is one with which we all live constantly. The pounds come on so easily, but they're so hard to take off. I only wish I could give you a Total Diet so the pounds could fall off effortlessly. Weightwatching is part of that life-struggle, one of those nonfun challenges. Apparently, there is no easy answer.

The experts say that being overweight cuts my life expectancy and robs me of energy. Besides that, it makes me feel depressed. That's my main motivation to keep the pounds off. As the lady said, the key is "in my head." If I don't want to change, I won't. If I want to change, then there is hope.

Lose your excess baggage, if you can do it. And if you positively can't because of a glandular disorder or whatever, then accept that fact about yourself and get on with living.

Who Nose?

Pounds aren't the only weight we carry. There are as many problems as there are people. One problem that pops up again and again is how to accept an ugly feature or physical impairment.

A lovely woman expressed regret that she had not had her nose reshaped when she was young. Now in her adult life, she still felt self-conscious over her big nose. She looked attractive to me, but I could tell she was acutely upset. I told her, "If I were you and felt that miserable I'd have it fixed even now." She did. Her plastic surgery was expensive, but to her it was worth it.

Karen, a thirty-seven-year-old mother of three, had felt shortchanged ever since high school because of her small breasts. She found it very difficult to accept herself. When she went out, she dressed up and wore a padded bra, but for her husband she felt embarrassed. "How can I be a 'smoldering sexpot' when I am utterly flat-chested?" she asked. "I am always too tired to feel and act loving and sexy. Do you think my feeling tired is psychological since I'm so self-conscious about my nonexistent breasts?"

Many other women have written similar letters telling of their despair and inferior feelings in a breast-conscious society. They all feel cheated and unwomanly.

Karen's problem was not so much in her husband's attitude toward her as in her own attitude toward herself. "Being tired" was her escape. As a mature woman, she didn't expect perfection, but her breasts (or lack of them) had become an issue and that was affecting her married life.

We live in a world where hair transplants, contact lenses, and nose jobs are now commonplace. Karen sought medical advice and her doctor suggested breast implant surgery to increase her bust size. She discovered that for her it was medically possible and financially feasible, so she had the surgery. Later, she wrote again to say for the first time in her life she felt "like a woman." She had begun to act like a woman toward her husband, and naturally, he responded.

Whatever you can do to help your self-image, do it. Your doctor can tell you what's possible and what isn't.

But know in advance that surgery or contact lenses or even a new body *per se* won't cure your problems. External improvements can't even insure a super attitude on your part, but any improvement is a step in a forward direction.

Changing one's attitude, however, is sometimes as effective and much less expensive than surgery. Paula also felt her nose was too big for her face. She kept apologizing to Bob for it, until one day he said, "I love you just the way you are. I *love* your nose. You're beautiful. Now stop insulting my taste."

She was thrilled that he loved her just the way she is, big nose and all. Now she wouldn't dream of changing it.

My Body, My House

Every woman knows she must some day grow old and lose the bloom of youth. Yet when it begins to happen, she registers shock. Wrinkles appear overnight. She sees the law of gravity pulling on her underarms and chin and everything below the chin. Who would have ever thought it could happen to her?

Proverbs chapter 31 describes God's Total Woman. One of her chief characteristics is "no fear of old age"[3] because she follows His plan for her, day-by-day. He makes life so great there's not much time to fret about the bags and sags, much less time to fear them.

In my case, there are many things I can never change about myself, but I'm not going to waste any time wishing I could. I accept them (sometimes over and over) and then I can get on with the important business of giving, loving, and bringing joy to myself and others. As Jesus said, there certainly is more to life than the body![4]

While my girls and I were talking about life one day, I told them, "Your body is actually a shell, a 'house' you wear. The real you which is inside your body will someday leave. So if anything happens to your body, it won't affect the real you. Even if you were in an accident and your arms or legs were cut off, the real you would still be intact inside."

That afternoon Michelle saw a midget at a carnival. I explained, "God has given that man a very short body to wear while he is here on earth, but the person inside him is exactly like you, with the same feelings and desires."

Since Michelle was about the same height as the midget, she watched him closely and then asked, "Mom, will I be a midget, too?"

"I don't know," I answered. "You might, and if so, then that's God's plan for you. That's the kind of 'house' He planned for you to wear."

To me, that's very comforting. Knowing that God designed my house takes great pressure off me. I am not going to fight His design. Someday we'll be free of these bodies and their diseases and limitations, but for now we're stuck inside. I'll change what I can and accept what I can't.

Flying High

Finding yourself may take a long time, but in the process you'll discover some delightful fringe benefits. First,

you'll find you are no longer jealous of others' achievements, but will be truly glad for their good fortune. You
will want other people to achieve their full potential and
will rejoice with them when they do. You will be thrilled
about their being them and joyous about your being you!

Life is so short. Begin today to develop your talents
and personality. The ache of inferiority is a tragedy and
a waste. Find your style and your rhythm in life. As you
accept and then develop your special individuality, you
will be energized, positive, and enthusiastic. Finding
you will send you soaring into the vibrant joy of self-
expression.

2 Where Am I Going?

Before any woman can be effective in the kitchen, in the community or in the business world, I believe she must know *who* she is and *where* she's going. First, accepted; then directed. The *going* is the goal.

Viktor Frankl, the European psychiatrist who spent three grim years at Auschwitz, wrote about the prisoners who died mentally before they ever died physically. The reason—they had no goals.

"One prisoner felt as though he were marching to his own funeral," Frankl wrote in *Man's Search for Meaning.* "His life seemed to him absolutely without future. He regarded it as over and done, as if he had already died—a feeling of lifelessness."

A man or woman without goals to pursue begins to relive the past and to wish for "the good old days." If he loses faith in the future, he soon loses touch with reality and is on the edge of giving up.

Charles Colson, the former White House lawyer, tells of a similar experience during his brief stint in jail for the Watergate-related "crimes."

"Like an invasion of locusts, the empty hours eat away at a man's very being," wrote Colson in *Born Again,* describing the prisoners who spent hours on menial tasks like shining a belt buckle over and over. "Soon there is near-total disorientation: staring at the clock, its hands never moving; losing track of time and place."

Many women live a prisonlike existence in their very own homes, with no meaning or reason to life. The only difference involves staring at a television set instead of a clock.

Dare to Dream

The Reverend Steve Brown of the Key Biscayne Presbyterian Church once said, "If you have no place to go and no plan to get there, you'll stay lost." The Bible says, "Where there is no vision, the people perish. . . ."[5]

Where are *you* going? Think about it. Evaluate your daily life. Are you expressing your personality and talents creatively? If you had one year yet to live, what would you accomplish during those 365 days?

How do you set a goal and actually follow through in spite of all the pressure against you to succeed? I recall one woman, who had settled into a comfortable middle-aged rut, and was stunned when her husband started taking flying lessons at age fifty. Rather than stay home and sulk, this spunky wife determined to overcome her fear of flying by taking lessons herself. Months later she wrote, "I can't believe this is really me, but I am taking my written exam for my private pilot's license next week!"

Prior to the birth of Michelle, it was my fate to lie in a hospital bed for three long months. Flat on my back with no visitors allowed, I stared at the bilious green walls day after day. Through all those endless hours, I longed to do something constructive such as write a book, but I was too drugged to even read, let alone write.

At last the new baby arrived and we came home. Now my life was in time slots of making formula, feeding Charlie and Laura, and restoring order to my home after my long absence. What a ludicrous time to write a book, but while knee-deep in diapers, that's when I decided to do it.

Bypass the Barriers

For most people, the two main barriers to setting realistic goals are the ruts and the roadblocks. Millions of good intentions have gone down the tube because of these two simple but devious culprits.

Barrier #1: The Ruts

Harriet Habit stays in her rut and won't break out for anything or anyone. Years ago, Harriet's groove turned into a rigid rut which cannot or will not be changed. Her favorite excuses against any new ideas are: "It's not on my road," or, "I've always done it this way," or, "I'm too busy." She never takes *I can* for an answer.

How much easier it is to stay in a rut than to try to break out of it. Someone has defined a rut as "nothing more than a grave with both ends missing." Igor Oganesoff, one of the producers of the CBS "60 Minutes" documentary summarized the Total Woman concept as "breaking the cycle of a rut."

Can you develop your original talents and express your potential while trapped in a rut? I can't. For me the only way out is to climb out and blaze a new trail.

When I finally decided to write a book, Harriet Habit quickly reminded me, "You're too busy." She whined, "You're out of your mind. You've got meals to cook and diapers to fold and kids to train. Why, you don't have time to breathe!"

I began to agree with Harriet. Then I remembered, there is never "enough" time.

Barrier #2: The Roadblocks

In addition to Harriet Habit, Phoebe Phobia strikes fear in the heart of anyone determined to create and accomplish. She intimidates subtly. She takes true facts and distorts them with fear. Her roadblocks shriek *Danger* when there is none. "I'm too old for that"; "I'm too young"; "too short"; "too dumb."

Psychological barriers, if you believe them, appear to be real and enslave you even before you start. Sometimes your best friends may tell you, "You can't do it," and if you listen you'll find they are right. You can't.

Many well-meaning friends have Phoebe Phobia riding their backs. They are quick to put down any new idea for multiple negative reasons—one being lack of knowledge on their part. As Dr. Clyde Narramore says, "People are always down on what they're not up on."

While I was trying to write, I ran smack into a roadblock which said, "Stop! You're not a writer." The small print in the corner read COURTESY OF PHOEBE PHOBIA.

The sign was so impressive, I sat down and watched it for a long time. At last I remembered my journey to new horizons and, disgusted with the delay, I scaled the barricade, kicking out a few neon bulbs as I went over.

I recharted my path and began to churn up the road, when suddenly another foreboding roadblock appeared. It stopped me dead in my tracks. In capital letters, it read WHAT IF YOU FAIL? The small print read PAID FOR BY THE FEAR OF FAILURE COMMITTEE.

From out of nowhere Phoebe appeared and leered, "Don't go on. Come on back." Knowing that nothing guarantees failure like fearing it, I held my ground. "I prefer to go on," I said, and I hurried away from her.

Picture It Done

In James Michener's best-selling novel *The Source,* Mr. Zodman returned to his homeland of Israel. On the tour his guide wanted to show him the ancient ruins. Instead, Zodman wanted to see the newly planted national forest. He had helped pay for those six million trees. "The ruins have been dead for thousands of years," he said. "The trees are alive today."

I realized one real danger in keeping my eyes on the long-range goal. If I wasn't careful to look around, I might bypass the trees and beautiful sights along the way. Pressing on to the goal, yet savoring the days on the path, is one of the secrets to life. I had to maintain that delicate balance of living in the moment and seeing the trees, but at the same time steadily moving toward the goal.

I stopped and spread a picnic under the trees. After a refreshing interlude, I hit the trail again.

Jack Nicklaus, golf's great winner, once revealed a secret of his magnificent putting. "I've never missed one in my mind," he said. "The ball doesn't always go in the hole, but I didn't miss it."

Once you set your goal, then picture it done. Without this finished picture in your mind, you'll give up halfway. With it, there's no limit to what you might accomplish.

Ada Soubirou learned to play the piano without a piano. Even though her parents couldn't afford a piano, they provided their little girl with music lessons. Ada returned home each week with her lesson book in hand and seated herself at the window sill where she "practiced" for hours every day. By carefully tapping out the notes on the sill, she "heard" the notes in her mind and learned her lesson. Today, Ada is Laura's piano teacher and is an outstanding recording artist.

Back on my road, late one night I reached my destination and there I saw it. My book, completed! As I opened the pages, suddenly my eyes blinked. I looked down; in my hand was a pen, and resting in my lap was a pad of blank paper.

I had fallen asleep without ever writing a word. Though I felt exhausted from my mental struggle on the road, I had seen the book completed in my mind and was all the more determined to make my dream come true.

From Here to Eternity

Once a goal has been set, the next step is planning the strategy to reach that objective. Seeing is believing; doing is achieving. Map out a specific course. Having a plan gives the motivation to follow through.

One common trait of every successful woman is organization. Plan ahead before you jump in. A former president of DuPont pointed out, "One minute spent in planning saves three or four minutes in execution." Those three or four minutes add up over a day and a year and a lifetime. A Total Woman sets aside time to plan carefully. She makes sure her life is counting not just for time, but for eternity.

A woman wrote from Maine, "It is midnight on January 20. I am writing down on a memo pad what I want to accomplish tomorrow. What a long list and what a beautiful feeling. It feels almost as if it is half done."

And it is.

After you have planned your work, then work your plan. My plan consists of *prayer* and *perspiration.*

Prayer is the most essential ingredient in starting any new project. When I ask for God's direction each morning, I believe that He will answer. He has, He is, and He will.

King David prayed, "Seventy years are given us! And

some may even live to eighty. But even the best of these years are often emptiness and pain; soon they disappear, and we are gone. . . . Teach us to number our days and recognize how few they are; help us to spend them as we should."[6]

If you have never prayed before, don't be afraid to start. If you have tried to get your act together, but you can't fit the pieces in place, tell Him about it. Even if there's only time for one word, He will hear that urgent, heartrending *Help!*

The second *p* in working my plan is *perspiration.* My goal is inspiration; working toward the goal is perspiration.

Work is the world's easiest escape from boredom and the only surefire road to success. Thomas A. Edison said, "I never did anything worth doing by accident; nor did any of my inventions come by accident; they came by work."

Panic Palace

Phyllis Diller, while talking about her disorganized housekeeping, quipped, "I'm eighteen years behind on my ironing. There's no use doing it now—it doesn't fit anybody I know!"

The one problem which seems to hit American women the hardest is simply too much work and too little time.

A secretary from Arizona wrote, "There is no time left for any personal pleasure after my nine hours at the office and another eight spent shopping, cooking supper, taking care of the house and Fred. What can I do?"

First of all, acknowledge that there are only twenty-four hours in a day. Every day. That fact can't be changed. The only exception I know is Proverbs 10:27: "Reverence for God adds hours to each day."[7] Zounds! Imagine that. And do I ever need the extra hours!

Next, it's helpful to admit that your work load and responsibility increase with age. If you are one of nearly half the women in the country who works outside your home, your work load is automatically doubled. Furthermore, with promotions come ever greater demands on your time. Dr. Samuel Greenberg, University of Miami psychiatrist, says, "The higher up you go [in business], the more hours you wind up working. As many depressions are brought about by promotions as demotions." The great demands on your time mean tremendous pressure on you and naturally less time for your family. What a real threat to family life!

The only variable then is how you choose to use the twenty-four-hour days allotted you. Time is precious. In the words of William Penn, "Time is what we want most, but alas, we use worst." Benjamin Franklin advised, "... do not squander Time for that's the stuff Life is made of."

A civic-minded girl friend told me how she hates to sit through meetings every month. "They're such an endless waste of time. I feel so restless—as though I'm not supposed to be there at all." So many women spend so much of their lives doing things they really don't want to do. God's plan for your life is fulfilling, not agitating. I don't know anyone who isn't busy, but busyness may be nothing but spinning wheels or going in circles. A Total Woman is result-oriented, not activity-oriented.

President Eisenhower said, "I have found that the urgent is seldom important and the important is seldom urgent." If you are a slave to the urgent, you will never have time for the important. You may think at times there's a campaign afoot to keep you from your priorities. That's not a campaign, that's only life, so determine to stick with the important.

Worst Things First

In *The Total Woman,* I referred to a daily organization plan designed for U.S. Steel by a management consultant, who received $25,000 for inventing it. In a nutshell, the plan is doing "first things first." List all your immediate responsibilities and work on them in their order of importance.

I find that it helps to prepare your list for tomorrow's jobs tonight. This way your subconscious mind is preparing for action even while you sleep.

Defuse the pressure spots by tackling worst things first, early in the day when you're fresh. Delaying action on those worst things only increases your tension and makes the problems loom larger. Sometimes facing a problem squarely makes it diminish in size or even disappear altogether.

Husbands appreciate the $25,000 Plan and often

adapt it for their daily schedule. Both of you may wish to make a joint list of the goals you're working toward as a team.

Even my girls are learning to make their priority lists the night before, so that the most important things in their young lives are accomplished. Practicing the piano is one of Laura's top priorities. When she's working on a piece for a recital, that takes precedence over playing with girl friends. She is learning to postpone present gratifications for greater future rewards.

The secret to attaining goals is working a little bit on it each day. You can't move a mountain in a day, even if you work until you're exhausted. Pace yourself. Exhaustion inhibits your work. Don't stay on the goal until you're bleary. Break down your big projects into little projects.

If the baby has been crying, you may need diversion to renew your creativity. Play with the baby. Take a walk, take a shower, take a nap. If you think you might sleep for hours, set the alarm.

Years ago I knew that a ten-minute nap with my feet elevated on a pillow made my eyes sparkle for my date. Years of marriage and babies had blotted that beauty tip from my brain until recently. I remembered and tried it. Besides the sparkle and glow, I find a reservoir of strength. So stretch out and recharge. The relaxation in a ten-minute nap is revitalizing. You might even write that nap slot on your $25,000 Plan.

I wish young mothers with babies could realize that those hectic demanding days and nights will pass. When you think you are going under for the third time, remember that your babies and your schedule will improve. Soon the children will learn to dress themselves, feed and entertain themselves, and within a few years, go off to school.

As they grow older, you can then exchange ideas adult-to-adult. One day you will desire their companionship above all others. But now, while they are in your hands, you are building the very foundation of their lives.

You haven't much time.

Roll, Baby, Roll

What happens when the best laid plans are suddenly scrapped and you find yourself facing new circumstances? A lady once asked me that question. She said she had served on enough committees to fill a book, and telephoned enough people to make a directory. But when things fell apart one day, she sat down and wrote, "If I were in your course right now, my grade would be *F.* Today I failed, flunked, and gave up the ship. I mean when you are on Plan *X* at dinner time, and fall into your bubble bath at 11 o'clock P.M. with tears having ruined your mascara, it's really foolish to kid yourself into thinking the day could be salvaged."

I understand. I hardly ever experience a Plan *A* day anymore. Life and its upsets seem to gain momentum as I grow older. But I am much more able to cope when I have a workable plan. When the bottom drops out and everything is in chaos, I have two choices: Go bananas or be flexible enough to adjust to Plan *B* or Plan *C* or *T*. I'm learning to make things that go wrong part of my plan. Daily crises are another of life's challenges, but my attitude can make the overcoming fun, wherever I am.

The Bible says a merry heart does good like a medicine.[8] When I have a merry heart it's easy to speak kindly to others and cope with Plan *B*.

One day, some years ago, I determined to have a "merry heart" even if it killed me. Of course, by starting out with an attitude like that, it almost did. I was already behind the eight-ball by breakfast when the baby knocked a pie off the table. Then the cleaners lost Charlie's best shirt. At noon, disgusted, discouraged, and hungry, I headed for the school. While returning home with a carload of little preschoolers plus my baby, the car stopped dead in 89-degree heat in the middle of five lanes of traffic.

I wanted to cry. Then I remembered that I was setting the atmosphere for everyone in the car, so instead I laughed—rather hysterically. The little ankle-biters looked at me surprised, but then they too started to laugh. As we all held hands and raced across the traffic, we laughed. As we trudged for help, we laughed. As the police arrived, we laughed. I told my little charges brightly, "We're having an adventure!"

One said, "You're crazy!" but I believe that they will always look back on that day as a highlight of junior kindergarten.

A merry heart helps melt away the troubles. People

need to laugh at themselves—at the crazy quirks in life. Somehow it helps.

You can tell your husband your problems, not as great tragedies, but as jokes. When you tell him, "You wouldn't believe what happened today," you both can laugh at it together. There is always enough that goes wrong that you don't have to look very far for a good laugh!

I like the quote of Buffy St. Marie, "I was an oak. Now I'm a willow, I can bend." A sign which hangs over a friend's sink reads SUBJECT TO CHANGE, LORD.

His ways are not our ways, though that's difficult to understand at times. When I can't see the reason why, I claim the verse, "This is the day which the Lord hath made; we will rejoice and be glad in it"[9] . . . *anyway.*

Remember, when things go wrong, only your plan has failed; *you* haven't.

1. If you haven't cleaned your windows lately, the Dirty Window Quiz might help you get started:

A. What one person comes to your mind when you read the word *angry?* Who best fits the description of the word *depressed?* Cheerful? Sad? Bitter? Which of these people would you like to be stranded with on a lonely isle?

B. Describe yourself in a one-word epitaph. Are you grouchy or kind or hostile or fat? Choose your own word.

C. How do you think your husband and/or friends would describe you in one word?

D. Does your friend's or your husband's description of you in question C, match your own description of yourself in question B?

Are you "The Great Pretender"? Do other people know who you really are? Do you?

2. Draw two perpendicular lines down a sheet of paper to make three columns.

A. In the first column, list your most pressing problems.

B. In the second column, write what you wish would happen to each problem (if wishing would do it).

C. Finally, in the third column, write the action you plan to take to make your wishes come true!

3. List the ten people who have most affected your life. Then describe in one word the strongest quality or trait of each of these people. You may then want to adapt some of these traits for yourself.

4. Write a book. Tell your life story. Keep a pad and pencil at hand all day and by your bedside. Jot down thoughts as they come to mind. Otherwise, you'll probably forget—or stay up all night trying to remember.

Part Two
The Joy of Giving

3 Accept

"Last Thursday was New Year's Day," the football widow's letter began. "I am still seeing football helmets in my dreams after watching Bowl after Bowl after Bowl." Her husband, she said, is also a golf nut and every other kind of sports nut. Not only that, he's an aggressive businessman, who takes his office work with him wherever he goes. She wrote to ask, "What can I do to find my husband again?"

I identified with her plight. When Charlie and I were dating, we attended every football game and golf tournament that came to Miami. I loved Charlie and most of the things he enjoyed, but I just couldn't tolerate sports events night after night.

I consented to go to the games simply to watch the people. I did enjoy seeing who was wearing what as the throngs passed by like a huge fashion show. During our first date (at a ball game naturally), I was aware that Charlie was staring at me. As I turned to him, he pointed to the playing field and deadpanned, "That's the game down there."

Months passed. I made a mental note of what to do if we ever got married. Charlie's interests definitely needed broadening in other areas besides sports. I would make him more diversified and well rounded.

After we were married, I realized to my dismay that Charlie's interest in sports had turned into a passion. Our romance and communication soon diminished, and Charlie glued himself to the television set to escape my harangues. I was so jealous of TV football I couldn't see straight.

Resentful and frustrated, I decided to set a goal of my own. I took on the project of correcting Charlie of all his faults. He was a fine young man and didn't have very many faults, but there were a few idiosyncrasies. I knew I could round off those few rough edges, and then he would be just perfect!

The best way to start my project, I thought, would be to *point out* his faults. So day after day, for six and a half years, I enumerated his faults very explicitly so he could see what to change. But not once in all that time did he ever change one thing.

The weekend TV football games disturbed me most of all. I couldn't imagine anyone being interested in the Southwest-Northeast-Aggie-Normal-Whatever game. One weekend, Charlie watched five consecutive

TV football games without moving. I even thought about having him declared "legally dead"!

Thinking positively, I then seized upon my opportunity of having him settled in one place. At least I could talk to (or at) him. During the games I reminded him of his household duties. "Take out the garbage," I told him during one crucial third-down play. "It's time for dinner," I yelled. "Go get some milk; we just ran out."

Usually these requests went unnoticed, but once when I quietly changed the channel (thinking he was asleep), he exploded, "What are you doing?"

"You've watched enough TV for now," I scolded, regaining my composure. "Now will you please go to the store and get some milk?"

"I heard you the first time, and the second," he said as he jumped to change the channel back. "Will you please stop nagging me to death!"

So that's it, I thought later—years later—to be exact. *To him, nagging is saying it more than once!* I didn't mean any harm by nagging. I was only trying to be *helpful.*

"Nagging," according to the Bible, is like a "constant dripping,"[10] a Chinese water torture. Charlie was experiencing pure misery.

The Proverbs say a husband would rather live on the roof than inside his house with a nag.[11] My husband, who had turned into a silent, preoccupied stranger to escape The Nag, was ready to get the ladder.

In addition to nagging, the second plank in my platform was to remake Charlie into my mold. I began by setting up a picnic for Saturday afternoon, the day of the season's opening game.

That idea wasn't met by roaring enthusiasm, but I didn't give up. I kept on suggesting alternatives.

After six years I realized I wasn't making much progress, but I still wasn't discouraged. *Just give me ten more years,* I told myself.

I discussed my problem (or rather my "challenge") with a friend over lunch one day. She gently told me, "Marabel, I also tried for several years to make my husband over, but then I decided I didn't *want* him to be like me."

In working on my MHO post-marital degree (Making Hubby Over), I was driving a deep wedge between Charlie and myself.

Some friends dropped by one evening and Charlie told them sarcastically, "Marabel always treats me like a king." Then he bent down to the floor and snapped his fingers, "Here, King! Here, King!"

I finally got the picture.

Nick O'teen

Judging from the mail we receive, there must be thousands (no, millions!) of other sports nuts across the land. The complaints come from wives who don't share that same enthusiastic love for any kind of game.

(By the way, I have become a sports nut myself since I took an interest.) But if your husband is a sports nut and you don't like ball games, I know your problem. Of course, there are scores of other problems that wives complain about, such as a husband's smoking. Whether you happen to be married to Joe Jock or Nick O'teen, and you don't like what he's doing, what may I ask are your alternatives?

Pick one or more:

1 OPENING STATEMENT: Tell him, "I don't like your smoking" (or whatever it is).
2 ONCE MORE WITH FEELING: Tell him again, slowly and deliberately, "I-don't-like-your-smoking."
3 SCREAMING MIMI: Scream, "I hate your smoking!"
4 *YOUR* HEALTH: Cough and fan smoke, then leave the room gasping.
5 *HIS* HEALTH: Send him AMA cancer warnings anonymously.
6 SUGAR SUBSTITUTE: Hide his cigarettes and replace with candy ones.
7 BRUTE FORCE: Snatch away his cigarette the next time he lights up.
8 FROZEN SILENCE: Don't talk to him or grant any marital favors until he stops.
9 ALL OF THE ABOVE.

All of these steps are merely attempts to cause your husband to change his ways. If any of these attempts work, that's great. But they usually don't, do they? Then what are your alternatives?

As I see it, you can either (1) make yourself and your husband miserable for years by trying to force a change against his will, or (2) you can accept whatever he's doing that's bothering you.

The principle of accepting another person is basic to any human relationship. If some habit of your husband or your friend seems to irritate you, that may be a clue that you're not fully accepting that person. Some examples:

Minnesota Fats.   A Midwest housewife wrote about her aversion to fat people. Her problem was her overweight husband. He had gained sixty pounds since they were married, and all of it was in his tummy. "Nagging hasn't helped at all," she said, "but I don't know if it's possible for me to change my attitude about fat people."

If she can't change him, and can't change her attitude, the tension and weight will only continue to increase.

Car Freak.   A young wife complained that her husband constantly worked on cars day and night. "I don't mind the cars," she wrote, "but lately Ron doesn't know when to quit. He's been staying out until midnight every night now for six months and even all night some nights. It's always the same old excuse."

Normally, the options are (1) change him if possible, or (2) accept him if not. In this case, there might be a third alternative. Some night she might personally check out Ron's "body shop."

On Call.   Many women married to doctors or dentists have the problem of an unpredictable schedule.

Some husbands are "on call" nearly every night. One frustrated dentist's wife wrote, "Often the telephone rings five times after midnight, and out the door he goes to see someone who has carelessly knocked out his teeth in some weird accident. I'm really beginning to resent my husband."

I feel she really resents the callers and the schedule, but she is blaming her husband for the situation. If his job requires on-call duty, I can appreciate how difficult her life is. But so is his. The resentment will soon eat her alive unless she learns to adjust to his schedule.

Free to Be

Whether you're married to a sports nut, a doctor, or a work-a-holic, the problem is the same—what are you going to do about what hubby won't change?

If you find you aren't having success in changing your husband's (or your friend's) #1 fault, may I recommend the second option. Accept him the way he is, with it. That suggestion may cause tremors in your nervous system, but it may be worth a try if all else has failed. Here's why.

First of all, that negative habit of your husband may not be a *fault* at all, but rather a *love*. A golf widow said she had tried everything imaginable to keep her husband home on weekends, from screaming and crying, to loving and seducing, but nothing had worked. "If this situation is my fault," she asked, "what more can I do? Isn't it possible that my husband could be at fault?"

It's possible, but it's more likely that it's nobody's fault. He just loves golf. No fault—just love.

Second, if you suspect your husband won't ever break out of his rut, face that fact and accept it. Newspaper columnist Sydney J. Harris said, "The most difficult and most essential task in marriage is learning which defects must be ignored and accepted in the other partner. Most unhappy marriages are created by trying to change what cannot be changed."

Third, when you accept your husband just the way he is, a weight rolls off your shoulders. No longer will you be leading the revolution or heading a correctional institution. Once the burden is lifted, your sleepless nights will improve. So will your days.

Fourth, acceptance really does work wonders. A woman wrote to me complaining about her husband's drinking. Completely fed up, she finally moved out with her baby on New Year's Day. "I wanted him out of my life forever. I hated him and everything he stood for. I filed for divorce."

After several weeks, she reconsidered and went back home for one last try, but against her better judgment, she began to nag again. He said, "If you keep pushing me, I'll only drink more; but if you shut up about it, things will work out."

She shut up, and believe it or not, he stopped. When she began encouraging him instead of nagging him, she found a new man. Not another man—but her own husband!

Of course, I realize that not all husbands may respond

favorably, but I do know that acceptance frees a man to be himself. A pilot said it this way, "I wonder how many men could make their wives the happiest women in the world, if only their wives would *allow them* to give the best of themselves."

A skeptical wife tried "accepting" her husband and wrote me a month later. "Would you believe," she bubbled, "in just two days he was opening up and talking. He hasn't even turned on the TV. Not only does he take out the garbage now, but he also replaces the liner! I know that doesn't sound like much, but it means a lot to me."

A fishing widow wrote a similar story. Her husband said, "It's more fun to fish on weekends than be with you." When she quit her crabbing habits, he changed his fishing habits. "My husband has come back to life! Now we fish together, but he even forgot the fish were there for four days straight. A miracle? I'll say!"

It's no fun being the husband of a nag. A divorced husband wrote that he could never relate to his wife, nor could he get the point across that she was nagging. According to his story, she wouldn't let him be independent, which was his nature. "I never listened to half of what she said, because about half of it was nagging. If she hadn't nagged, we would be happily married today sharing the joys of each other and my child, which I deeply regret that I am unable to do."

Taming of the Shrew

Now that we've considered the perils of nagging, I think it's only fair to confess that I haven't kicked the habit completely myself. Nagging for me is still a nagging problem. Sometimes it scares me to see how quickly and frequently I tend to lapse back. Occasionally, I even nag "after the fact."

One night Charlie and I went to bed very late. We had both worked hard all day and fell asleep the second we hit the bed.

Suddenly, out of my deep dream I heard a dog barking right underneath the bedroom window. We don't have a dog, but I imagined that some stray had treed a squirrel or cat.

I shook Charlie who was still asleep and said, "Charlie, please go stop that dog!" He muttered something incoherent, stumbled out of bed, pulled on his pants, and went out the door.

The barking stopped. Charlie came back inside, climbed into bed, rolled over and was out like a light.

About twenty minutes later (who knows how much later at that time of night?) I was reawakened by the same barking—and again, right under our window.

I jabbed Charlie and told him where to go. Again in the darkness, I heard him mutter something, pull on his pants, bang into the dresser, and grope his way to the front door. Then I heard a rock crash against wood. "Yelp!"

Then silence, *sweet* silence.

Charlie returned, pulled off his pants, got into bed without a word, and dozed off at once. I took a little longer.

How long I slept that time, I don't know. But the thing

that I had feared came upon me. "Arf, arf, arf, arf."

By this time, I was frantic. I was so exhausted and had hardly slept at all, and now it was almost morning. My nerves were screaming.

Jab Charlie. More muttering. Pull on pants. Bang dresser. Slam door. Rock against wood. Wood against wood. "Yelp!" "Yelp!"

Silence.

"Yow!" That's where Charlie stubbed his toe on the sprinkler head.

"Arf, arf, arf, arf."

Door slam. Enter Charlie. Limping. Muttering. Pants pulled off. "Ow! That's it! I'm going to sleep!"

"Arf, arf, arf, arf, arf. . . ."

I didn't sleep the rest of the night and the dog didn't stop the rest of the night. I was so tired and so mad at Charlie and/or the dog, it never occurred to me to do anything to silence Fido.

The impossible dream. The inevitable dog.

When I came into the living room at daybreak, Charlie lay sound asleep on the couch with a pillow over his head. "Well," I began, "why didn't you stop that crazy dog? Why didn't you do something instead of coming in and going to sleep?" I was very tired and resentful. I crabbed until he left for work and picked it up again when he came home that night.

Charlie was also exhausted from the midnight dog chase. He slumped in a chair and said, "Please. Sit down and listen. Point number one: I tried to shut up that blasted dog last night, three times. I threw rocks at him.

I threw sticks at him. I chased him around the yard and stubbed my toe. I didn't sleep all night either. Then, I stumbled in to breakfast to find that the barking hadn't stopped yet!

"Point number two: Look! I tried to shut that mutt up last night. Now, it's over. So will you please stop nagging me after it's over."

I was nagging "after the fact," and I had to agree; it was so pointless. It isn't easy for me to keep quiet. I do bite my tongue a lot, quite a lot. That isn't to say I never express myself and my feelings to Charlie. I do. But after a while, I just try not to bug him any further. If I have an emotional need to nag, I call a friend and she doesn't take it personally. If she's out shopping, she suggested I call "Time and Temperature"; they'll listen to anything!

Acceptance can do what nagging cannot. Tammy Johnson wrote to tell how she had nagged her husband unmercifully, but some months after the divorce, she called him to apologize for her part in the breakup. He was amazed—so amazed that he began to date her again, and after some time, asked her to remarry him. She said, "I won't be nagging this time around. I'm using the Bible for my guide to be the best wife possible. I just know he will feel his second choice was the best!

"Every good wife needs patience and I intend to perfect that trait. The clouds have moved away from the sun. Because of my total acceptance, I'm finally able to see the rainbow."

4 Admire

It was Friday afternoon, and Mr. Feelin' Low glanced at the wall clock with mixed emotions. After a long, hard week he was glad that Friday had finally come. He looked forward to a hot shower and a hot dinner, but he dreaded facing the cold wife.

Friday afternoon meant a long weekend at home, just trading one headache for another. *Something's missing,* he thought. *Is this all there is?* Loneliness rolled over him in waves. Somewhere, someone must admire him, even if his own wife didn't.

Stardust

Thoreau said, "The mass of men lead lives of quiet desperation." Tonight, all over America people like Feelin' Low are grappling with the same needs, the same loneliness, and the same quiet desperation. Starting from earliest childhood and continuing all through life, a man is recognized and applauded for his accomplishments, and who doesn't love that type of admiration? Women do, too.

Look at any scrapbook. What's on the first page? A diploma from the Cradle Roll class, or a perfect spelling test with a big gold star. Pasted in the pages are high-school Honor Roll certificates and athletic awards and ribbons and yellowed clippings. Many husbands keep their letter jackets all their lives.

If your husband was a Big Man on Campus, he probably has all sorts of trophies, stars, and other special memorabilia. Have you noticed how a person will do almost anything for a star? Football coaches now award little stars to outstanding players after each game. If you watch a Saturday afternoon college game, you'll see the stars plastered on the helmets. Imagine that! Grown men with stick-on stars! But everyone loves admiration, and somehow it's a fitting reward for those grueling hours and weeks and months.

The military services all reward accomplishment and rank with stars and ribbons. Business organizations and civic clubs hold award dinners, Salesman-of-the-Month contests, and Plumber-of-the-Day prizes. All these various modes of admiration are designed to reward and motivate to even greater levels.

A man tries to fill that crying need for admiration in many ways. If he's a headhunter in the Amazon jungle, on his palm-frond walls he displays visible proof of his achievements—shrunken heads, boars' teeth, and horns of ferocious animals that he personally has slain.

If he's a headhunter in the Atlanta jungle, he displays stuffed fish, moose heads, certificates of appreciation, and the union runner-up bowling trophy.

Status books, banking on the vanity of men who love to see their name and accomplishments in print, have become a lucrative business today. These book publishers entice members of a certain group with a lofty title, and then attempt to sell copies back to the same people. Titles may range from *Who's Who in Iceland* to *Who's Who Over There*.

But a man longs for respect and admiration from his wife more than any other person. You can transform your husband from a "Who's he?" to "Who's Who on Main Street" by a few genuine words of encouragement. You can make him your star, tonight.

Tomb of the Unknown Husband

In one large city, twenty-four-hour recordings now turn out tender messages for lonely men much like Dial-a-Prayer and Dial-the-Weather. A sultry woman's voice croons, "You're the most exciting man I've ever met." After a pause for effect, she continues breathlessly, "I wonder if the real woman in your life realizes how lucky she is." Softly, she adds, "I do!"

In the same way that many women sometimes feel insecure about their looks, so do many husbands. As your husband grows older, his need for admiration grows greater. Gravity takes a toll on his body, too. With a balding head and protruding paunch comes the question, "Does she think I'm handsome?" Even if he still looks like a Greek god, he may feel insecure unless you encourage him verbally.

One of my favorite cartoons shows a couple on the front doorstep in the morning. The wife is in robe and curlers, and the husband is aimed toward the street. The forlorn husband's caption reads, "Give me a little push." A fresh, sincere compliment would do it!

So often I too need a little push. We all do. When Charlie tells me I've done a good job, suddenly I'm motivated again. I have that same power to motivate him. What could be easier than expressing my love with a little verbal sunshine? Many a woman has written to tell of her husband's overwhelming response to a compliment she gave at the end of the day. At the beginning of the day, at the end, and all through, a man can't have too many! A man, a woman, or *any* person!

What motivates a man to be responsible and to succeed in his ambitions? What one incentive will help a man remain stable, faithful, and loving to his wife and family?

For some, the satisfaction of accomplishment is a compelling motivating force. Others are driven by a great pride in their vocation. They thrive on keen competition and love the challenge of giving their all. But let's face it, for most men life is a daily grind. There is neither exciting competition, nor any particular pride of performance on the job. It's just the same old grind.

In poetic terms, admiration can put back the skip in a husband's walk, the sparkle in his eyes, and the flutter in his heart. He will dare to dream again and believe in his abilities, because you've told him you do.

I heard of one husband who became a work-a-holic because he was literally starved for admiration. When his wife took the first step and remarked on how handsome he looked leaving for work, he stopped and said, "Do you realize that's the first compliment I've had in twenty years?" How sad. He even remembered the last time, and had been keeping track all those years.

If a husband needs admiration, why is a wife sometimes reluctant to give it? Why is it a threat to admire the man she married? The kindest words about a person are usually spoken after he's dead and isn't around to appreciate the eulogy.

In the words of humorist Berton Braley:

Do It Now

If with pleasure you are viewing any work a
     man is doing,
   If you like him or you love him, tell him now;
Don't withhold your approbation till the parson
     makes oration
   As he lies with snowy lilies o'er his brow;
For no matter how you shout it, he won't really
     care about it;
   He won't know how many teardrops you have
     shed;

If you think some praise is due him, now's
the time to slip it to him,
For he cannot read his tombstone when
he's dead!

Me and My Ego

A wife has the ultimate turn-on for her husband's self-image, an act of kindness that takes less than a minute, and yet, so often she refuses to give it. Why? There are many reasons.

Busy Bea.   With so many other things to do, Busy Bea just doesn't have time. "I'm ticket chairman of the charity dinner," she said, "plus all my afternoons are spent en route to Girl Scouts, Little League, and ceramic classes. When I get home, I'm tired. I don't even want to talk to anyone, let alone sit around praising *him!*"

Me First.   Other women find it impossible to take the initiative. "Are you kidding?" Ruth asked. "What about him complimenting *me?* I'm doing research at the hospital. My energies are directed toward creating benefit for all mankind. Let him compliment me first."

Admire What?   Some women can't verbalize admiration because they actually can't see where to start. "Well, I don't know," one lady confided. "We just don't seem to have much going for us anymore. I mean, what would I admire if I wanted to?" I don't know what, but she must have seen *something* in him when she married him.

Super Stud.   Finally, some women refuse to give compliments because their husbands are already well aware of their own attributes. As one wife said, "I'm married to a very good-looking man who knows it! He's already stuck on himself."

On the NBC "Tomorrow" show, host Tom Snyder asked Bobbie Evans and me about that same problem. How could Bobbie compliment a star like her husband, Norm, then an all-pro tackle with the Miami Dolphins. Norm's schedule was six months of football, and six months of speaking engagements, and on his days off, he went fishing with "the boys." Norm had become a stranger to Bobbie. "I stayed so mad," she said, "I used to freeze the leftovers so he wouldn't have anything to eat when he came home. Compliment? His ego was too big already! Everybody always made such a fuss over his beautiful body; if I started complimenting him, he'd be impossible to live with!"

At a game one day Bobbie watched as Norm blasted through the line ahead of Larry Csonka (then a Dolphin). She suddenly realized that neither Csonka nor Bob Griese was giving him compliments like, "Wow, Norm, those are some shoulders you've got!" She also realized there were lots of chicks waiting outside every locker-room door, ready and willing to admire his body.

Then Bobbie decided she had better be the one. When she began to verbalize her feelings, Norm began to come alive. One night he told her, "Bobbie, not only are you my wife and lover, but you're my best friend!" And guess what? He even stopped going fishing every Monday!

Whether your husband is the YMCA Ping-Pong champion or the all-around handyman, he needs your support. He needs you to build him up. If he acts stuck on himself, he may simply be giving himself the reassurance that you are not supplying. Tact is the ability to see another person as he sees himself.

Pop Goes the Ego

I have observed that at any point in time I am affecting people around me in either a positive or a negative way. So is everyone else. I have also noticed that it's usually easier to be negative than positive.

We start out the day reading the horror stories on page one, and so often it's all downhill from there. Former Chief Justice Earl Warren said, "I always turn to the sports page first. The sports page records people's accomplishments; the front page has nothing but man's failures."

Clinical psychologist Chaytor D. Mason of the University of Southern California wrote, "Once, the press built heroes. Now it unmasks them."

During some winter games on TV, I was amazed that the producers chose to replay—not the rare moments of record-breaking performances and beauty—but the slips, the miscues, and the embarrassing moments.

An article in *U.S. News & World Report* entitled "The Vanishing American Hero," asks why global idolatry came to Charles Lindbergh and not to Neil Armstrong. "Why does Ruth still occupy an almost sacrosanct niche in baseball that is beyond the reach of Henry Aaron, a great hitter who broke the Babe's career record for home runs? . . . . In the place of enduring models such as Caruso or Chaplin or Pavlova or Ellington are found waves of celebrities as replaceable as a low-caliber TV serial."

The style of today is to tear people down. If words could wound, mankind would be in a mass intensive-care ward. One reporter admitted that she wrote her daily column with "a terrible pervasive cynicism."

Well, that's not for me! I prefer to look for the good news and be a positive influence in my sphere. This enthusiasm naturally carries over to wanting to be positive with my husband.

How to Make Your #1 Be #1

Have you ever wished that your husband might be the president of his company? Or the owner of his business? Or the best farmer in the county? Or the foreman of his shop?

You can have a part in possibly making that dream come true. Here's how to start.

1. *Be sincere in your admiration.*   The word *compliment* comes from a Latin word meaning "to fill up." Flattery or insincere praise only causes anger, but true admiration gives reassurance.

One lady, who didn't think her husband was particularly good-looking, began to look for things to admire about him. "I've discovered qualities I'd never thought about before. Now since I've been admiring him, he's become the most handsome man on earth."

2. *Admire his body.* See your husband as he sees himself. As he looked in the mirror this morning while getting ready for work, do you know what he saw? Not his pot and receding hairline, but a firm eighteen-year-old youth with a full shock of hair. As he admired that figure in the mirror, he growled inwardly, "You tiger you!"

He wants you to see that same tiger. Tell him tonight, "I admire your _____!" You may be surprised at the results.

A New York housewife of two short years admitted that her marriage was on the rocks, partially because of her. "I wanted this and wanted that, and so on—nag, nag, nag." She thought her husband was "skinny and disgusting, sitting glued to the television with a cigarette hanging from his mouth." But when she began admiring his favorable qualities, there were instant results. He quit smoking, gained twenty pounds, and "looks just great." She exuded, "We feel like newlyweds again, and the more I admire his new body, the more I find that life is full of surprises."

Another woman revived her husband with one measly compliment. He came home from work each night and put on the same old, knee-length, terry-cloth bathrobe, and then "dried-up" for the evening. She hated the robe and the way he acted. One night she told him, "If you didn't have such beautiful, sexy legs, I couldn't tolerate

that thing another minute." The next night her husband
was a new man in a new robe. "For a man who hadn't
even kissed me for four months," she wrote, "I was loved
three days in a row, and now he sleeps with his arms
around me every night."

3. *Admire his accomplishments.*   The principle of admiration is not restricted to husbands, but works equally
well with children, friends, and anyone you meet. When
a football coach was fired last year, one of his players
remarked, "He was too quick to criticize and too slow to
compliment."

A real estate developer in Florida desired to buy prop-
erty from a large landowner, but she had not been able
to meet the owner personally. Finally, a ten-minute
meeting was set for her to present her proposal. Knowing her time would be short, she arrived early with her
presentation well prepared. She was escorted in to meet
the elderly gentleman at the appointed hour. Seeing a
stuffed owl on his desk, she exclaimed, "Mr. Jones, what
a beautiful owl!" Mr. Jones smiled, and then leaned back
and began to talk. Two hours and a lunch later, she
emerged with a contract on a large tract of his land.

This principle of admiration works in business as well
as in the home.

Vocal Bouquets

It was the last day of school and the Little Red-Haired
Girl was oblivious to Charlie Brown. She didn't know he

existed. "You know why that Little Red-Haired Girl never sees me?" Charlie lamented to Lucy. "Because I'm nothing! How can she see me if I'm nothing?"

"Why don't you want to talk to me instead of the Little Red-Haired Girl?" Lucy demanded. "I was the Christmas Queen. Huh? Charlie Brown. Why? Huh? Why?"

Later that afternoon, he found a note taped to his locker. "I like you. Signed, THE LITTLE RED-HAIRED GIRL."

Charlie Brown clicked his heels and shouted, "Oh, boy, nobody will laugh at me now. I can't wait till September!"

Your husband wants to click his heels. Don't make *him* wait till September. Give him a reason to get up tomorrow morning!

Once a wife begins to admire her husband out of a heart of love, the results are far-reaching.

A lady from Texas wrote, "My husband who is 5 feet 6 inches thinks he's 10 feet tall every time I tell our friends about his recent promotion."

A widower also wrote to tell how admiration begets admiration. His wife's loving attitude had left a precious memory and he listed all her attributes. Intelligent, with a master's degree in chemistry, she was kind, gentle, and had fun whether she was working or relaxing. She always praised him, patted him on the back, and let him know how much she loved him.

"I tried in every way I knew to return that love," he wrote. "She made that part so easy. I still miss her and her loss is the greatest I've ever experienced. For thirty-

two wonderful years she kept handing me vocal bou-
quets which put me on Cloud Twelve. We never had
time to think of divorce. We were too busy being
happy!"

5 Adapt

"I came terribly close to ending my three-year-old marriage," the letter began. "My husband stated correctly the other day at dinner that he and I should go into the yard, take separate corners, and start butting our heads together like two billy goats, because that was exactly what was happening."

Three years ago the minister had declared that "the two became one," and that's when all their problems began!

How could two egos—one wife plus one husband—"become one"? Which one survived the merger? Why did holy wedlock turn into unholy deadlock?

Before marriage, many a woman imagines that her husband-to-be will always agree with everything she says and never challenge any of her ideas. Unfortunately, while she is thinking it's *her* show, he's thinking the same thing!

After marriage a couple may encounter for the first time the Conflict Monster, a creation of their joint efforts, who feeds on any two opposite opinions. Two different opinions can arise on any and every subject—and usually do: where to live, how to spend the money, how to raise the kids, where to go for dinner, who sleeps late on Saturday, and on and on.

As a result of the Conflict Monster, husbands and wives everywhere go their separate ways instead of going and growing together. Can two opinions be fused into one, and if so, how?

The challenge in marriage is to blend these two egos so that the two go down life's road together with a minimum of friction. Adapting is simply a method which solves the problem of two egos battling in a marriage. The Scriptures which gave us the principle that a house divided against itself cannot stand[12] also said, "Wives, adapt to your husbands."[13]

Head Knocking

The concept of a wife "adapting" to her husband is probably the most difficult part of life for me. The concept may also be one of the most controversial portions of the Bible, from which I learned it originally. I claim no pride of authorship on this issue, and I must confess that I sometimes don't strictly follow the scriptural principle—often to my sorrow. I believe the Bible is truth, and I know that my strength, my joy, and direction come from reading that Book daily. Therefore, I can't ignore the principle of adapting, even though at times I could scream rather than live it.

The very word *adapt* is an explosive word. I find that it almost always brings a sudden and rather violent reaction, depending, of course, on the present company and her degree of hostility.

I have been criticized and ridiculed for even suggesting the subject. A psychiatrist told me that criticism often comes from women who are personally embittered over an unhappy marriage. Their hostility is merely redirected at me when the suggestion of submission is made. I can understand their feelings.

In other cases, criticism is based on a misunderstanding of what adapting actually means. It has nothing to do with a woman's career. She may compete with anybody in any realm. She may be the company president with the highest salary. The principle of a wife's adapting to her husband as stated and restated throughout Scripture is limited only to her husband, and not to all men in general. This principle—more than any other—may be the one that makes or breaks a marriage. So let's consider this most important, yet most misunderstood, marriage concept.

Compromise or Conflict

One Friday afternoon Charlie told me he had planned a fishing trip with some friends the next day. I had already arranged to play tennis on Saturday to practice for a tournament the next week.

Question: What should I do? Should I tell him, "Your fishing trip sounds terrific, dear. I'll cancel my tennis game right away. What's up for me? May I come along and bait your hooks?"

No, no, a thousand times no! On that particular Saturday, Charlie fished all morning and I played tennis. We both did what we wanted to do. There was no problem of adapting since Charlie hadn't even invited me to come. Each of us simply did our own thing.

If Charlie had wanted to play tennis that day with me, or if I had wanted to go fishing with him, fine. So long as both he and I were both doing what each of us wanted to do, and neither of us cared what the other was doing, there was no problem of adapting.

One week later. Same scene.

It was Friday night. I was excited over the tennis tournament scheduled for the next day. At dinner, Charlie said, "By the way, the Parkers are in town for two days."

"Oh, great," I said.

"I told them we'd go fishing with them tomorrow morning," he said.

Oh, no, I thought to myself, trying desperately to keep my composure.

Question: Now what should I do? Should I tell him, "Yes, dear, I can't think of anything I'd rather do tomorrow. I was just wondering what excuse I'd give to get out of that dreadful tennis tournament"?

Maybe he had forgotten that I had entered the tournament six weeks before, but I wanted to *play*. I thought for a moment, wondering how I should respond. Then in as sweet a voice as possible, I exploded!

The first stage in the making of a controversy was reached. We locked horns. Charlie wanted me to go fishing Saturday, and I was determined to play tennis. The Conflict Monster was formed. The ingredients: two or more people had two or more ideas about a certain course of action which did not agree.

Teeing Off

A discussion ensued. In fact, for the next two hours we discussed the problem, neither of us budging an inch.

Actually, the word *discussion* was rather a loose description of our activities. We argued. We fought clean. We fought dirty. I tried to make a deal. Why not play tennis in the morning and fish all afternoon? That wasn't possible. I tried every form of compromise I could, but this night there was none.

The thought of adapting to his way flashed through my mind and I quickly blotted it out. Our positions became all the more polarized. I wanted to play tennis, but I also wanted unity.

Charlie went to the bedroom and then took a long shower. About twenty minutes later, he said, "Look, Honey, I know how much you want to play tennis. The Parkers will understand, and I understand."

Because Charlie withdrew his request for me to go fishing, the principle of adapting never came into play,

mainly because I wouldn't let it. The argument was settled at the give-and-take compromise level. *He* compro-
mised.

Often this compromise stage for us is very spirited and
heated and extends for long periods of time in our struggle to resolve the problem. Of course, Charlie doesn't
always concede at this level by changing his mind.

I remember a similar deadlock last Christmas over
what color our Christmas tree should be. Charlie wanted
to spray it with white flocking; I wanted the natural
green look.

It ended up white.

I didn't adapt very well to Charlie's decision. He just
sprayed it over my vehement objections. I was mad before it was sprayed; I was mad after it was sprayed; and
I was mad while it was being sprayed.

Finally I got hold of myself in our bedroom, and gave
me a good talking to. *Look,* I said to me, *Charlie is more
important than a tree. What difference does it make
what color the tree is?* (The time spent in adjusting to a
White Christmas was considerably more than this one
paragraph, but I will spare you my hours of emotional
anguish!)

How Far West?

If you could hear me at our house, you'd probably
think, "What a loud mouth!" Like most people, I, too,
have an opinion on just about every subject. Charlie and
I talk and talk and sometimes shout. I believe in equal

treatment and playing fair. I believe in the flag, mother-
hood, and compromise. We try to work out all our problems by compromise, but sometimes compromise just
won't cut it.

Others have admitted problems in this area, too. For
example, Arlene Francis told me of an impossible conflict that occurred early in her marriage. Her husband
said he might be transferred to Los Angeles. She was
young and ambitious and only wanted to be in the
theatre, which was based in New York. She didn't want
to go to the Coast and miss any opportunities. In the
midst of her pleading not to go, her husband asked,
"How far west would you go for me, Arlene—Sixth Ave-
nue?"

The question was either L.A. or New York. In her case
"compromise" was not possible, either in Saint Louis or
Phoenix. By the way, her husband was never transferred
and they remained in New York.

If two solutions are possible, the problem is often resolved before it gets this far. But if only one solution is
possible, what then? When conflict (Step # 1) can't be
resolved by compromise (Step # 2), then what?

When a couple reaches a fork in the marital road and
the decision can't be postponed any longer, usually there
are only two ways left—"my way" or "his way."

What a Difference a Tree Makes

Before the advent of Total Woman, Charlie and I dis-
agreed over whether or not to cut down a scraggly, bot-

tlebrush tree in front of the house. There wasn't room for a middle-of-the-road accommodation solution. It was either the tree or no tree. I knew he wanted it, and I hated it.

One day when he left for work, I took his hatchet and cut down the stupid, scrawny tree. With the lyrics ringing in my ears of Frank Sinatra's "I Did It My Way," that night I confessed to Charlie I had cut down his favorite bottlebrush tree. Actually, I didn't have to confess it. He saw it when he came in the house. It was weeks before we were friends once again.

The consequences of doing things "my way" can be grave. If the wife accepts an out-of-state job offer, while her husband stays home, her move may cost her a husband. In my case, the consequences weren't as grave simply because the alternatives weren't as grave. When I cut down the tree, I was only doing what I had done for six years—my thing. It wasn't a male-female thing at all, it was merely two egos in conflict—but my way was lonely.

As I continued to cut down other types of trees in our marriage, I was more and more lonely and unhappy. Demanding my own way every time became obnoxious —even to me. I wasn't happy even after I got what I wanted, and I certainly wasn't happy at the prospect of a divorce. "My way" was a one-way street. What was the remaining alternative?

The Holy Scriptures give specific instructions to wives: "Be subject—be submissive and adapt yourselves—to your own husbands."[14]

This principle has its roots deep in the Judeo-Christian heritage, starting with Genesis chapter 3. The husband was the divinely designated priest of his family. The responsibility for leadership of the family rested on his shoulders alone. The passing of thousands of years has not changed the authority of the Scriptures or the validity of this principle.

I find, however, that it's much easier to talk about what a wife *should* do than to actually do it, especially in this area. To paraphrase Shakespeare: If to do were as easy as to know, paupers' cottages would be princes' palaces.

Like women everywhere I react rather violently at times to the idea of adapting to my husband. I know the principle so well, but so often I conveniently skip over it for two reasons.

First of all, I ignore the principle because I'm a stubborn, opinionated, sometimes-hothead with a mind of my own. Before I was married, I lived alone and supported myself for almost nine years. I loved my independence and being my own boss, and disliked the idea of having another person tell me what to do. Whenever anyone tried to impose his will on me, my natural inclination was to resist. I had my "rights." I feared being restricted and trapped. Even now, after twelve years of marriage, those feelings still flash through me during times of conflict.

Second, I resist adapting because I feel my way is the best way. Often it really is, and that's what makes it all the more difficult.

But no matter how I dislike the idea of adapting, I am

certain that in the scheme of God's plan, my responsibility to God and my husband is to follow his lead. As much as lies within me, I try to do it.

Fortunately for me, the principle very rarely applies. Charlie and I work out most of our conflicts at the Compromise Level. Sometimes that takes five minutes, and sometimes five hours, and sometimes five weeks. There are very few situations we can't resolve, but when they do arise, I have a method available for settling them.

The principles of adapting and accepting (which was considered earlier) are kissin' cousins. One principle involves accepting another *person,* and the second involves adapting to *his way.* Adapting occurs by a predetermined decision on *my* part to go his way. If I adapt only out of an ulterior motive, I'm manipulating. Sometimes when I choose to adapt, I am furious, and Charlie knows it. But nevertheless, adapting is my voluntary decision.

Little Red Personhood

An irate woman wrote me recently to ask, "Why are you trying to impose your flea-brained ideas on us American women?"

I explained, "This principle of submission was not my idea, so don't blame me if you don't agree with it. I don't like the idea myself, at times, but I must consider the Source. I'm not forcing you or anyone else to adapt; I'm simply sharing how our marriage has improved."

If you and your husband have another way of dealing with problems that can't be resolved by compromise, that's great. I've heard that some couples agree to use other methods, such as flipping a coin, or alternating the final decision between the spouses each time they disagree. If such methods as "keeping score" or a "game of chance" work for you, then there's no problem for you anyway. All your potential conflicts will be resolved at the Compromise Level. You can skip the rest of this chapter and go straight to Sex 301. But for me, I find that a prearranged plan of settling disputes is orderly and eliminates confusion when it is applied.

Later on in the letter from the same irate woman, she claimed, "Your book should be called *The Total Slave.* Subservience is nothing but slavery. You're preaching 'doormatism.' Total nonsense! Total hypocrisy. Why not be a Total Person? 'Me, Tarzan, You, Jane' is a long way from a mature, adult, loving, sharing relationship."

Submission is *not* subservience. Subservience connotes an *involuntary* action against one's will, such as slavery, whereas submission is voluntary. Whenever I *choose* to adapt to my husband's plan, it's my decision, not Charlie's. If he threatened me or forced me bodily against my will, that *would* be slavery, or even rape.

I must admit, however, that when I first read the admonition "to adapt" in Scripture, my reaction was the same. I feared what might happen to me if I ever did it. My husband might become a dictator and walk all over me. But that's never happened once in my marriage. In fact, I was recently asked about an example of adapting in my own life, and when I thought about it, I couldn't recall the last time I had adapted.

You see, once I determined in my own mind to adapt

(when all attempts at compromise had failed), I found
that my husband was not unreasonable. In fact, frequently he would change his mind and do exactly what
I had wanted to do all along.

Loving the Unlovely

So often I have been asked, "Doesn't the husband
have responsibilities, too? What about him? One-sided
giving is not fair."

I agree. For six and a half years I reminded my husband of his responsibilities. I repeatedly told him how I
thought he should be contributing to our relationship.
The only problem was he didn't contribute.

Julie Twilley said, "Is it really so much to ask a woman
to take the first step in breaking down barriers in her
home? Why should it be a threat for a woman to give
love to her husband?" Once I took that first step in an
effort to save my marriage, to my wonderment Charlie
became an incredibly responsible husband!

A young divorcee wrote that she was planning her
second marriage but wanted to know exactly what
adapting would cost her. "I really do care and want to
please my sweetie," she wrote, "but how can I carry all
my responsibilities and then turn around and purr like
a kitten? I guess I am waiting for him to offer to do some
of these things. Where does pleasing him end and you
begin?"

Adapting involves giving. Adapting is not giving for
the sake of getting; that's *manipulation.* Anyone can
spot a phony. Don't you know when you're being

manipulated? So does your husband.

Marriage is not a 50–50 proposition. Anyone who has been married knows that at times *both* spouses must give more than 50 percent to make a successful marriage. The First Lady Betty Ford once said that marriage is a "70–30" proposition. Jesus went even further, exhorting to give 100 percent with no thought of what you'll receive in return.[15]

New York psychologist Robert Mercer says that adapting is simply The Golden Rule. "What ye would have others do unto you, *first* do ye unto them." He notes, "What a privilege and advantage it is to be the one to *initiate* a cycle of behavior. This is for strong and honest women, not for weak, conniving, manipulating, hostile, or defiant ones."

Lots of strong and honest women have written to tell how they initiated a cycle of love. "Like all newlyweds," wrote Ellen from New York, "I had trouble by the double trying to adapt to the real person I married. I admired my husband and accepted him, but I didn't adapt to his ways. I couldn't cope because he wouldn't change."

In the months that followed their divorce, Ellen had second thoughts about Barry. She wrote, "I put down my pride and asked him for forgiveness." Three weeks later they were remarried.

"Now my husband is trying very hard to please me!" she wrote. "Our sex life has really improved, too, except I must tell you it is completely dead now. Last night while waiting for him to come home I put on the sheer nightie he loves, makeup which I rarely wear, soft music, and candlelight. Well, I could never express how excited he got. We went to bed and, snap! he has two broken ribs. We are in our early twenties, so we have lots of years to make up for the six weeks while his ribs heal. Thank you again."

A lady from Virginia said, "If we lost everything tomorrow, we would love being together and starting all over and enjoy getting here just as much the second time around." After fourteen years of marriage which "seems like one," she told how her heart still jumps when her husband comes home, and she really lets him know it. He is color-blind so she lays out all his clothes every day without feeling or acting like a slave. "My husband couldn't find another woman that would be as good to him," she continued. "He knows it and he tells me so in many ways. He is home every night or out with *me*. Now which is the bigger fool—my friends who tell me I am a doormat or me?"

It was Helen Keller who said, "Life is an exciting business and most exciting when it is lived for others."

In *The Art of Loving*, Erich Fromm wrote that "giving is often misunderstood as 'giving up something, being deprived of, sacrificing.' " Instead, he describes *giving* as "the highest expression of potency."

"In the very act of giving," he writes, "I experience my strength, my wealth, my power. This experience of heightened vitality and potency fills me with joy. I experience myself as overflowing, spending, alive, hence as joyous. Giving is more joyous than receiving, not because it is a deprivation, but because in the act of giving lies the expression of my aliveness."

6 *Appreciate*

LOST: ONE HAPPY, SWEET BRIDE, ONE GIRL
WHO THINKS I'M WONDERFUL AND
TELLS ME SO

HER CHIEF CHARACTERISTIC: APPRECI-
ATION

AMPLE REWARD OFFERED: BY ONE DIS-
COURAGED GUY

I received this postcard from a husband in California.
It was anonymous. Not that the name mattered. Count-
less husbands across the land could have composed this
ad.

So often people tend to take each other for granted.
When they experience special treatment at frequent in-

tervals, soon they begin to *expect* that they should be on the receiving end, not the giving. They lose their attitude of gratitude.

The story is told of a generous movie star who bought four Cadillacs for his family at Christmas, one each for his mother, father, brother, and sister. When the presentation was made procession-style, complete with windshield signs and huge bows, the response from his family was completely unexpected. No appreciation, only grumbling. Then they began to attack, "Oh, what a waste! This is ridiculous!" On and on they admonished.

Finally the benevolent donor couldn't take it any longer. He slipped out the back door and caught a plane to Los Angeles, where he told the limousine driver, "Just drive me around for three days. I don't know if I'm ever going back home to those ingrates."

Here was a man who left his family on Christmas Day to fly halfway across the country to find an understanding, appreciative stranger who cared.

Last summer, Dr. Johnson and his wife attended a medical convention. From the time they left home until they returned, his wife complained nonstop. "The room didn't have an ocean view; the service was terrible; the personnel was surly; the food was lousy!" And she acted as if it was all her husband's fault. His eager, romantic feelings that had been building for weeks went down the drain. He vowed to himself he'd never take her on another trip.

Giving Thanks

While in a southern city recently, Charlie and I were invited for dinner, with several couples. We were introduced, then sat down and began to order. Mr. Burns, one of the guests, said in a matter-of-fact tone, "I've been here before," and then ordered the chateaubriand, the most expensive entree on the menu. I looked at the price and cringed for our host.

When the dinner arrived, Mr. Burns took one bite and declared the meat was tough. "John," he said, "the food here is just not what it used to be. The best place in town for steak is across town. Now *there's* a place you ought to try sometime." I cringed again.

As I watched Mr. Burns push his plate aside leaving more than half of his steak untouched, I marveled at his lack of sensitivity. Never once was a word or even a hint of thanks ever considered.

Bobbie Evans said, "There is an attitude which does more to keep you well than any other. It is thanksgiving. Gratitude seems to stimulate the life force and keep it flowing."

Appreciation has no relation whatsoever to your personal evaluation of something; for example, whether the steak was especially good or especially bad. Instead, it is your positive response to a favor another person has done for you, such as an invitation to dinner. If the steak is truly inedible (and that usually isn't the case), don't blame your host or hold him responsible for taking you out to the restaurant. Don't blame your husband for buying the meat for dinner last night. Either your host or your husband tried his best. The blame (if you find it necessary to "fix" blame) lies with the restaurant or the cook or the cow. Once a person makes a special effort to do a favor for another, it is the height of insult and rudeness to fail to express your appreciation.

While I was visiting with a friend, her husband came leaping in the front door waving some tickets in his hand. "Honey, look what I just got! Two good seats for the big play-off game Sunday. It's been a sellout for weeks."

His nonathletic wife was completely unimpressed and blurted out with utter disdain, "Oh, ick!" He wilted on the spot.

Point 1: Never fail to express appreciation for a favor. You can thank him for what he did, even though you may not like the gift.

Thike You

When husbands and children observe Mommy being appreciative, they "catch" that marvelous trait themselves. We try to encourage our little girls to be aware of other people's feelings.

Just before Christmas vacation in the first grade, Laura asked for some notepaper and pen and disappeared into her room. When she came out she was smiling and gave me a note to send to her teacher. It read, "Dear Mrs. Weber.   Thike.you.for.teeching.me.so.meney.things.I.-like.spleing.and.ridding.and.A.   Thike.you.   Love, Laura."

Point 2: An appreciative spirit cannot be taught, it must be "caught."

Forty More Mommies

I have been training my girls to do the household chores as soon as they are old enough. I don't want them to learn the hard way (after marriage) or under pressure. On the day I gave Laura her first ironing lesson and a pile of handkerchiefs, I kept pushing her to stay at it all morning, "Look, Laura, watch me. This is the way. You've got to learn to iron. I'm preparing you for life."

My little tomboy, who would rather lie upside down, reading a book, said, "Please, Mom. Do me a favor. Save the sermon. Don't prepare me for life!" My preaching was definitely not motivating her.

Dr. Clyde Narramore recalls when he was a little boy with five brothers, his mother used to tell him from time to time, "I wish I had forty more sons just like you." He felt so important and truly believed his mother wished there were forty more Clydes running around.

One morning I looked out the window to the patio and saw Michelle busily sweeping leaves off the porch. I watched with amazement and amusement. Amazement —because she did it without being told that day, and amusement—because the broom was twice as tall as she was!

I went out to give her encouragement. "You're so responsible, Sweetie. I'm proud of you. In fact, I wish I had forty more little girls just like you." She looked at me with surprise and then swept all the harder.

The next day, as soon as she came home from school she headed straight for the patio again. After a while I went out to watch. She stopped, and looking up, said, "Mommy, I wish I had forty more mommies just like you."

I thought, *Oh, how darling.* Then Michelle, popping my pride, added, "If I had forty more mommies, we'd *really* get the work done around here in a hurry!"

Point 3: Criticism wipes out motivation, but appreciation works wonders.

Terrific But Specific

When Laura made the Honor Roll in the fourth grade, I told her how pleased and proud I was of her achievement. Michelle, standing nearby, looked downcast and asked gloomily, "Aren't you proud of me, Mommy?"

I stooped down and put my arms around her. "Michelle," I told her, "I certainly am proud of you."

She looked unimpressed and asked, "For what?"

Point 4: In giving appreciation, be sincere and specific.

Christmas in July

In the same way that adapting is a cousin of accepting, appreciation is a kissin' cousin of admiration. Admiration involves praise for another person's abilities or accomplishments, while appreciation is "thanks-giving." Both of these principles apply not only to husbands, but to anyone, even an ex-husband.

Kathy has been divorced for three years and wrote to tell about her newfound love life. She works during the day and has little time to spend with her children, so she tries to make that time quality time and fun. She told me some of the ways they celebrate together.

"Being both parents isn't easy, but there are many rewards when love and faith are allowed to grow daily. Every day we all take time to appreciate one of God's beautiful creations.

"My boyfriend Bill was born December 21 and during his childhood, neither his birthday nor Christmas was ever very special. So we all celebrate his birthday every month and we celebrate Christmas in July, with tree lights, presents, and the works. We even plant a tree in his honor on Arbor Day.

"As for my ex-husband, he and I talk about the children in a civilized manner. Because we are no longer working against each other, it's not uncomfortable for the kids and me to join their father and his new wife for ice cream after a PTA meeting. I have seen that it's possible to be a Total Woman even with my ex."

The principles that make human relationships run smoothly are as old as the hills, and yet I need to be reminded again and again.

A lady wrote from Kansas City, "I've given a tablespoon of appreciation and my husband has given me back bushels of love! And how! Wow! I've given a few words of admiration and now he's talking a leg off me with his plans and hopes and somedays and, golly, it's great!"

Appreciation *motivates!* Husbands learn by example. Whether your husband is a superstar or a little guy, his needs in this area are great. Even a headliner needs praise for motivation, but all the more so the unheralded type who will never make the headlines. His life consists of working an assembly-line job all day and feeding three hungry kids at night. He works hard. He's faithful to his wife. He pays his bills. He plays with his kids and he loves his God.

That's news!

A lady wrote, "I have had the attitude 'who needs him?' but now I realize how terrible I'd feel if he felt that way about me. Do you think it's too late?"

No.

Assignment

1. This week celebrate Appreciation Awareness Week. Be aware of all of the little things each member of your family does, and personally thank each one.

2. When your husband is courteous, thank him for it. As a courtesy gesture on your part, acknowledge his *thoughtfulness.* Two of the most important words in marital relations are "Thank you."

3. If he does an odd job especially well around the house or remarks about his success at work, compliment his *accomplishment.* The five most important words in marital relations are "You did a good job."

Appreciation comes in two flavors—thanks and compliments.

Part Three
The Joy of Loving

7 Sex 301

"Here it is 2:00 A.M. and I just finished reading your book. Instead of reading so late, I realize now I should have been in bed with my husband! I want to start making $A+s$ instead of the $C-s$ I've been scoring for three years."

Many a woman has expressed a concern and desire for a revved-up sex relationship with that man who shares her life and bed. During twelve years of marriage and the advent of two hyperactive boys, one weary wife became so exhausted that her sizzle gradually ebbed away. "My frustrated husband knows that somewhere down inside of me is the sexy wife and lover he had before," she said. "He is an incurable romantic who wants our entire life to be just like the honeymoon."

And from Dallas, an excited newlywed exuded, "I

never heard all this before. Thank you for teaching me something my mom never cared enough to explain. I've had my first orgasm. Every woman should know what I've just learned—and is my husband ever happy, too!"

Fire Trap

Sex not only excites, but also comforts a man. This afternoon your husband may have an Excedrin headache. The pressures at work may have given him indigestion after lunch. Sometimes when his heart misses a few beats, or that ominous grip begins to tighten around his chest, a man begins to wonder if it's worth it all. How desperately he needs to be comforted, and how marvelously sex comforts. You can help soothe away his frustrations (and your own, too), as you begin to satisfy each other sexually. If *you* don't, someone else may.

A girl wrote to say she was deeply in love with a man who was fifteen years older than she. "I am wild about his body and would love to get him into bed. When I told him that, he said, 'I'm honored that you think I'm so attractive.' He also said he'd think about it.

"I would rape him if it weren't physically impossible," she continued. "Even though he has a wife he can't stand, dating is difficult. So the only time we see each other is after he leaves work. I would sincerely appreciate any help."

Help to break up a marriage? Are you kidding? How awful to have the wrong woman turning on the wrong man!

Sad to say, far too many brokenhearted wives learn too late about the "other woman." Many women have written, "I can't believe this is happening to me. My husband told me he's been seeing this other woman for almost a year. In my mind, I picture him comparing me with her, and I wonder how I measure up."

How does it all start? In a million different ways. Dr. Melvin Heller, a Philadelphia psychiatrist explains, "The erotic fantasies beaten into us by radio, TV, and newspapers create pressures that are impossible for many a middle-aged male to withstand. He's pushed to purchase a brand-new sex life and wife, just as he's pushed to buy a new car." Sometimes he feels no guilt, thinking it's the *in* thing to do.

The Other Woman

Wherever you live, "out there" is some little sexpot, looking wide-eyed at your husband. My sisters, how can I jar you from your lethargy? She's just waiting to get her clutches on *your* man, and although I don't think wives should be running scared, I do think we should wake up and be aware of the unscrupulous female who has no qualms about breaking up a marriage.

If your husband travels, he is especially susceptible to the lure of the soft, easy, and available woman. Men go where they are invited, and stay where they're well treated.

Wives sometimes moan, "What does she have that I don't have?" Maybe not too much. *She,* whoever she is, may not be very attractive or have a great figure. A husband probably wouldn't be caught dead with her among his friends, but when he has a need, she's there. She is very much aware of him and sees to it that he's aware of her. She hangs on his every word. She giggles musically at his jokes and coyly bats her lashes. She looks "alive" and sexy and eager.

While he was commander-in-chief of the German Army in 1937, Field Marshal von Blomberg fell in love with his secretary, Erna Gruhn, who had been a notorious prostitute in Berlin. Following a brief but torrid romance, they were married.

The news spread like wildfire among the ranks, and von Blomberg was given an ultimatum, "Divorce Erna Gruhn immediately or be removed from your post." The commander left his exalted position and chose an ex-prostitute above rank and fame.

Before he died, billionaire J. Paul Getty said, "I would give all my wealth for one successful marriage."

I don't believe most home executives realize the influence a woman has over a man. For that fair creature, a man will give up power and wealth. He may even give up all other women. But to *keep* him, a woman needs to know how to meet his needs.

Fight fire with fire. Your marriage may only be in the brushfire stage, but be assured of one thing. If your husband's sex needs aren't being met at home, his spark is still there, smoldering.

In discussing the "other woman," a widow wrote a marriage columnist describing the wives in her neighborhood:

BERNICE: Wears curlers twenty-four hours a day. Is a chronic complainer. By the time her husband comes home for dinner, she is staggering around the kitchen, stoned.

MARGE: Visits neighbors all day. No housework except on impulse, which is usually at night when husband is getting ready for bed.

EMILY: Weighs 280 pounds. Drops food on her chin and clothing. Her bosom looks like a snack tray.

LENORE: Has told the neighborhood ladies they are fools to let their husbands "use" them as substitute call girls. Describes sex as degrading.

"I am a forty-year-old widow," the lady wrote, "and have been propositioned by every one of their husbands. One soft smile, one wide-eyed, listening look, and I could be the Other Woman."

365 Ways to Fix Hamburger

Dr. David Reuben said, "Most men operate on a forty-eight-hour cycle—that is, they need sex that often to keep them on an even keel."

Your husband's hunger for sex is as gnawing as his hunger for food. But unlike stomaching hamburger every night, a man hardly ever tires of sex. Therein lies the secret of how a wife can keep him interested only in her. A wife has the potential to turn on her husband time after time for a lifetime, but like hamburger you may have to prepare yourself in a variety of different ways now and then. Like 365, or 183.

An ex-prostitute from Las Vegas wrote, "I am now very happily married. Now that I'm on this side of the fence, I realize that if more women would do their homework and take care of their husbands, there would be no prostitution.

"I want my marriage to work. And the only way I can make it work is to keep my husband babied, pampered, cuddled, loved, and interested in me only.

"These women who want to be free women can have it—it's a bore, alone, believe me. I am more liberated now than before. We have so much going for us I could shout it from the housetops."

When a man's got butter in the refrigerator at home, he won't go out in the street for margarine.

The Odd Couple

SCENE   Herman and Nellie watching TV
TIME   Eleven o'clock P.M.
KIDS   Asleep
PLACE   Living room

Herman starts humming his mating call, "Lover, when you're near me," and Nellie knows she's in for it. She scurries to the bathroom, dons her flannel pj's, and slaps a coat of mayonnaise on her face. Clip, snap, and two big rollers and pins are in place.

Relieved that the bedroom is still empty, Nellie climbs into bed. She snaps off the light, and adjusts her sleep mask. Her transformation into Nellie Not-Tonight was sudden but effective, and not a moment too soon.

Meanwhile back in the living room sits Herman Hot-to-Trot, thinking wistfully that Nellie is preparing for him. Shutting off the TV, he snorts a few times and paws the ground.

Nellie Not-Tonight lies motionless under the blankets as Herman comes charging into the bedroom and hops into bed. When poor Herman lifts the blanket, he takes one look at the sleep mask and thinks he's in bed with the Lone Ranger!

He wants and she wants not. It's a familiar scene. They have been there many times before. I'm not writing about the weirdos, but the normal-Nellies I have met personally and through correspondence.

Many, many letters have poured in from men voicing their longing desire. Expressing the ache he felt, one man wrote, "Mrs. Morgan, what you say is right! I love my wife, but in all these years, she has never responded positively to my sexual advances. I could write a book on her negative excuses, 'I've got a headache,' or 'We're not kids anymore,' or 'The children might hear us,' or 'I'm so tired.'"

Dr. Henrietta Klein, Professor of Psychiatry at Columbia University of Physicians and Surgeons in New York states, "A woman is perfectly aware that sex is a man's most vulnerable spot. He identifies it with power and virility. It's a macho concept to some extent, largely due to our culture. His ego is very much at stake. A man can even feel shaken in his masculinity, if his touch doesn't arouse the expected sexual response in his wife."

Most women respond sexually on the honeymoon and in the early years of marriage. But over the years the fire often dies as multiple kinds of problems begin to surface.

A sixty-seven-year-old man wrote, "My first marriage failed and the second is far from ideal. Our present marriage went pretty well until about eight years ago when rocks got in the mattress. Things have now deteriorated to the point that I feel I am living in a boardinghouse."

Another husband sent an unsigned letter from the Midwest. Two months before, he had left home to assist his son who was quite ill. When he went to kiss his wife good-bye, she didn't raise her head from the pillow. "It was probably just as well," he said. "If she had gotten up, she would have looked like Phyllis Diller going through a car wash."

The problems in sex are not always sex problems. While deep emotional deprivations may require professional counseling, a few common problems seem to plague the masses. The following examples are intended to give help and encouragement.

Miss Match.   Some women find it difficult to respond sexually because of problems during their childhood. Sally never experienced love from her parents. As she and I talked over lunch, almost immediately she began to blame her husband for the discontent in their marriage. "Mike doesn't talk to me or play with the kids. I feel shut out of his life. I'm just needed as a maid." As our conversation continued, she admitted, "But, he's always ready for sex, anytime and all the time. I really think he's *oversexed.*"

All through lunch Sally criticized Mike. Listening between the lines I could hear her saying, "Poor me. I'm married to a beast, a sex fiend. Men are such animals!"

When a man loves his wife, he wants to show her frequently, and he wants her to respond. He is especially pleased when she is fulfilled. In Sally's case, it was only when she realized what was causing her inhibitions—and was willing and determined to overcome them—that she was able to enjoy sex-time.

Satisfying both partners in sex is sometimes difficult to balance. One woman complained that her husband wants to make love at least once every night and once every morning. "I'm really not as willing as I should be, because I am always so tired," she said. "But I give in anyway, and because of this he thinks I don't like sex. He's right. I'm sorry this letter is so sloppy, but it's midnight and you guessed it, I'm tired."

He may be a sex fiend! But I just don't believe that most husbands fall into that category. Sometimes a husband with a normal sex drive is considered oversexed by a wife whose level is unusually low. Her level may have been diminished because of various reasons ranging from being tired, to malnutrition or hypertension from an erratic schedule.

Four-leafed Lover.   "How are you supposed to respond to a husband who grabs you every time you pass him?" asked a cute but worn-out mother. "He pulls at me when I'm trying to get the baby changed and the kids fed. What do you do when your husband comes home from work and falls right to sleep on the couch, leaving you with no companionship? How can you give your time to your husband, when your two-year-old and six-month-old are demanding your attention?"

Actually, this girl has an ideal situation. When her husband comes in and grabs her, she could drop everything and meet his needs; her children are too young to know what's happening anyway. Then she could let him sleep for the rest of the evening, while she tends to her own projects!

Last month a local press organization presented their Red Garter Award to The Total Woman program. In making the presentation, the following lyrics were written by Gerry Healy and sung by Eleanor Hart to the familiar tune "Four-Leaf Clover":

> I'm looking over a pile of laundry
>   that I overlooked before.
> Four kids have measles,
>   another the mumps,
> The sixth has a fever
>   and funny red bumps.
> It's no use explaining
>   my head's migraining,
> My back aches from scrubbing floors.
>   My man of the hour
> Can take a cold shower
>   that he overlooked before.

If you're married to Herman Hot-to-Trot, you could push him in a cold shower once or twice, but if he's as

red-blooded as most American husbands, you're going to
have a fantastic water bill!

Nympho Nellie.   Occasionally, the "want-to" sex ra-
tio is tipped the other way, and Miss Match is the eager
one. Sometimes when a husband has little or no interest
in sex, his anxious wife is jumping out of her skin in
frustration. Again, I'm not talking about the clinical case
of Nympho Nellie, but rather Herman *Not*-to-Trot.

"My husband says sex isn't exciting anymore, because
I'm always ready," wrote an eager woman from Boston.
"I'm all set to go at any time of the day or night, and he
knows it. When we hop into bed, he knows I'm hoping
and I am. How can I become unavailable?"

You might try the cold-shower trick yourself!

Another woman complained, "I always feel my husband is making love to me just because it's expected. He
says I'm oversexed. When I try to seduce him, he yells,
'Just leave me alone!' I don't feel like a woman anymore
at all and I resent him for this."

All over America this problem seethes. From Houston:
"Sometimes my husband races to the shower and into
bed, even before I can get the children settled. I try to
snuggle up but his pillow is over his head. He is satisfied
with sex once a month or even less. At the rate we're
going, by our tenth anniversary we'll be shaking hands
every once in a while."

Unless both partners are being satisfied sexually, one
partner may be crying out, "Hey, I've got needs! I'm
frustrated because I need you to need me."

Talking out the problem could begin to put the gears in motion, and perhaps one (or both) partners would benefit from professional help. The sexual union takes time to work on and work out, so don't feel frustrated if all is not harmonious immediately. Give yourself a chance. Learning to know another person requires much give and take, acceptance and sacrifice along the way. But do begin today.

Certainly there are many psychological and physical causes for sexual disorders. As you know, I am no doctor but I can report some rather amazing results from the application of Total Woman principles. Let me share one exciting story. Whatever the medical ramifications, this *happened.*

A middle-aged couple was distraught because the husband could no longer perform sexually. His wife knew he was upset, but when she tried to encourage him, he simply withdrew into his own shell. His doctor diagnosed his condition as a chronic disease which had caused his impotence. The man was truly devastated and fell into a deep depression.

His wife, desperate at the turn of events, came to a Total Woman seminar, hoping to find some help to keep her marriage relationship from disintegrating. Three days after the second session, the wife in ecstasy called her instructor. "I've been applying the principles for nearly two weeks, and I wanted you to know," she glowed over the phone, "the doctor is *wrong!*"

Myths and Misses

A plaintive cry came from a woman who could not erase the memories of her wretched childhood. She recalled how her mother had "entertained" various boyfriends, many times all night. At times the daughter would awaken to hear shouting in her mother's room as policemen carried away one of the boyfriends.

"I'm married now and very restless," she confided. "At night, it takes me forever to go to sleep. Since I saw my mother in bed with so many different men, I have lots of trouble with sex. I knew I would, but I don't know how to cope. How can I get rid of this mental block?"

Throughout this land of America the Beautiful there are many women who experience a true repulsion of sex, in some cases because of misinformation, in other cases because of bitterness or confusion. For example:

Miss Conception.   "The creative energy in man," her letter began, "should be used for sex when families are young, to propagate the race. Older folks should use this creative energy for the higher centers of the mind to create great achievements in the world of art, government, and science. Besides, did you know that sex may cause cancer of the cervix? Sex should diminish after middle age, so both men and women can grow more beautiful spiritually and less energetic sexually. Between you, Dr. Reuben, and Ann Landers, the flower of American manhood may be polished off before they are sixty."

Long live the flowers! I only hope her husband shares her same belief.

Mother's Watching.   "My mother always warned me that men were 'no good' and all of them had only one thing on their mind. My mother still haunts me whenever my husband and I make love. There she is in my mind's eye, sitting at the foot of the bed. Slowly I am gaining a different outlook on sex. Now I am ready, willing, and able to love my husband instead of him having a *human sacrifice*."

Another wrote that when she was young her mother said, "Sex is not nice, no matter how much you love a man." She could never forget that advice, even after she was married. "After I read your book," she wrote, "I regretted that I did not love, comfort, and adore him as I should have. But he says I'm a different woman in one week! Incredibly, as I read I laid down a great burden of inhibition and guilt and misunderstanding. I am free—oh, the joy of it all!"

Bitter Babs.   In addition to various misconceptions about sex, another barrier to a warm sexual relationship is bitterness from one or both partners.

A woman from Indiana said that her husband is the neighborhood grouch, "but the minute he touches me, I'm supposed to melt and fall into his arms."

Every woman knows that "touch" and resents it. Every woman also knows how to regulate sex like a female Santa Claus, depending on whether he's been "naughty or nice." But therein lies a danger. Regardless of who is bitter, using sex as a weapon or reward may backfire.

One man called his wife a "brick wall of rejection, who

pulls away from any kind of touch." She claims to have risen *above* sex, which is "the lower, baser, sensual nature. Besides, there is no such thing as a frigid woman, only fumbling, bumbling men."

Bad moods or disagreements do not necessarily mean the end of love. To the contrary, his bad mood itself may be the signal that he needs her sexual love.

A woman wants to make *up* before she makes love. Completely mystified by her indifference or outright hostility, her husband only knows he wants to *make love* in order to make up.

Cake for Bait.   A divorced woman in her forties told how she had dated one man steadily for a year and then he disappeared. After several months he came around, not to date but only to drop in occasionally for sex. "I felt like a puppet on a string," she wrote, "only being used as a sex partner. I finally said I wasn't going to bed with him anymore until he decided to make it permanent. I know I sound like a teenybopper, but I am so confused. I feel so sad and unhappy. I want to spend the rest of my life with him, but how do I catch him to do it? I feel that if he has his cake and eats it too, why should he make any commitment as far as marriage goes?"

Why, indeed? One of the main rewards of marriage is the ultimate prize. "I've got all the benefits of marriage without marriage," said one swinging single. "Why should I saddle myself with the responsibilities?" Some noble men do, but millions don't, to the endless dismay of the conned women. As the lady asked, "How do I catch him to marry me?"

What will she use to catch him? You tell me. Without the commitment in marriage—and a spiritual commitment at that—the evidence shows that sooner or later, and often sooner, the chant goes something like this:

> Loving me is a chore
> He says, "Sex is a bore"
> 'cause he's done it before
> And he don't want me no more.

Rod Cameroun poetically states it, "Sex is great, fun and wonderful, but it is intended for marriage only. Like a fire in the furnace that keeps the house warm and cozy, if it gets out, it can burn the house down!"

Yes, God placed bounds on sex. Sexual intercourse was His gift to married couples. But I hasten to add, if you didn't know, or if you knew and didn't care, God is willing to forgive you and give you a new start.

Sex 301 can be one of the most enjoyable and exciting parts of marriage—a constant learning experience. The purpose of this next section on sex is action.

Happy homework!

8 Wives and Lovers

Hey, little girl, comb your hair, fix your makeup,
  soon he will open the door.
Don't think because there's a ring on your finger
  you needn't try anymore.
For wives should always be lovers, too!
  Run to his arms the moment he comes home to
    you.
I'm warning you . . .

Day after day there are girls at the office,
  and men will always be men.
Don't send him off with your hair still in curlers,
  you may not see him again.
For wives should always be lovers, too.

Run to his arms the moment he comes home to
   you.
He's almost here.

Lyric by Hal David
Music by Burt Bacharach
© 1963 by Famous Music Corporation

The lyrics of "Wives and Lovers" by Hal David exhort
the everyday housewife to set the mood for love when
her man walks in the door.

Time to Get Ready

If a woman isn't in the mood for loving her husband,
only she can get herself in the mood. I made that remark
on the program *To Tell the Truth,* and panelist Bill Cul-
len said, "I think that's the nicest thing I've ever heard.
I've never *heard* that before!"

What happens when your husband is ready for love
and you've got the sexual blahs? Although loving him
doesn't turn you on at the moment, you can turn yourself
on, if you want to.

Want to? That's the secret. The purpose of this section
on sex is *action.*

Hundreds of reports have poured in from women who
wanted to share the results of their creative experi-
ments. To revive a sagging sex life, many wives began
their day by walking their husbands to the door and then
waving good-bye.

One husband caught sight of his wife waving, so he
stopped, backed up and asked, "What do you want?"

"Nothing," she smiled, "I'm just waving good-bye."

"I thought you were calling me back," he continued.

"No. Why don't you go now, dear," she said. Puzzled, but pleased, he left, turning around and waving to *her* until he was out of sight.

Another husband, whose wife usually stayed in bed until he left for work, was surprised to see her up and waving. As he drove away, he watched her wonderingly in his rearview mirror and plowed into a telephone pole!

Still another husband happily drove away as his wife waved and blew kisses from their second-story balcony. As she turned to go back inside, she saw the man across the street in his upstairs window, grinning, waving wildly, and blowing kisses to her!

Waving good-bye is such a simple act that only takes a few minutes, but the encouragement factor is enormous.

Spicy "sweet somethings" also help to liven up the scene. Kathy, a wife of six years, put this poem in her husband's lunchbox:

> Roses are red
> Violets are blue
> I feel kind of sexy
> Please come home at 2.

Kathy went shopping all morning. Her husband worked thirty miles away, so there was no chance he would come home before five o'clock. (At least, that's what she *thought*.) But when she returned home at 2:30, she found this note that he had written stuck in the front door:

> Roses are red,
> Violets are blue,
> I was home at 2
> Where were you?

"The unbelievable part," she wrote, "is that my husband is a contractor and has never come home in the middle of the day, but at 1:30 he simply said he needed to go home for a while! You can be sure I'll never 'cry wolf' again."

Caring and Craving

One afternoon I was peeling potatoes in my kitchen while being interviewed on a live radio call-in show. We chatted about marriage for a few minutes and then the interviewer asked, "How about giving our ladies an assignment, Mrs. Morgan? Something they could do right now and call in to report."

I suggested that the women in radio-land call their husbands and say, "Hi, Honey. I called to say I just crave your body. Hurry home tonight. Good-bye." The interviewer laughed, and within a few seconds his switchboard lit up. I never said another word for fifty minutes. Those women in that midwestern city bombarded the show with their husbands' responses. Some called to say their husbands were stunned. An older lady said, "Wow, what a day. Can't wait. I never said anything like that before!" Many husbands laughed for the first time in years. Even the interviewer's wife called. He said, "Stay tuned, the engineer is taking over!"

The final lady caller summed it all up very well. "I can't tell you everything he said," she giggled, "except he did say, 'It looks like it's going to be a good week-end!' "

I was thrilled because good weekends spill over into good weeks. Good weeks make good months, and good months make good years.

The Yogurt Connection

Columnist Erma Bombeck spoofed about the "crave your body" phrase. When an imaginary Janet called Jack's office, he asked, "What's this about craving a party? It's only ten in the morning."

"I didn't say 'party,' I said 'body' as in Burt Reynolds," she replied. "Come home early."

"Burt is coming to our house for a party?" he queried. "This piped-in music drives me up the wall. See you at five."

In real life, Marilyn didn't have the nerve to call her husband at work, so she sent him a note instead. She wrote out "I just crave your body" and buried the small card in the yogurt, his lunch for the day. At noon her husband dug into the blueberries and pulled out the soggy note.

He was disturbed to think that such a prank could

happen in a reputable yogurt company. He wrote demanding an explanation and enclosed the note.

In two weeks he received a letter which read, "Dear Sir, Although we are extremely interested in your body, we would never *crave* it."

A woman's call to her husband not only grabs his attention, but also shows she cares. One afternoon Harry's wife called him to say, "Hey, big fellow, bring your body home early. I've got a craving!" There was dead silence, then a roar of laughter from four male voices. His best friends were in the office at the time and they heard every word on the phone amplifier!

After she hung up, he grinned and said, "Eat your hearts out, you guys!"

Another part of a Total Woman's preparation for her man is the bubble bath at four o'clock, or just before he comes home. For working wives, the bath time can be adjusted to fit both schedules.

A bubble bath is a terrific therapeutic pleasure. You bathe out stress and bathe in health (or so I am told). Whatever the healing properties may be, I can vouch that the bath certainly does wonders for the psyche.

Occasionally make your bath a special event. Strew fresh flowers Acapulco-style, or float sliced lemons midst the bubbles. You deserve it.

Your bath can be your private mini-spa, soaking in mountains of foam. After you feel like a melted cream puff, wrap yourself in a giant towel. If you can spare the time, snuggle up in a chair with a book and a cup of tea for twenty minutes. The final effect is the same one feels at a spa, and not a fraction of the time and cost.

A number of women have even coaxed their husbands into a drift of bubbles, and it does wonders for them too. When he emerges all aglow, be his attendant, ready with the giant towel to wrap him up. This can also be an effective enticement for the man who doesn't want to bathe after a hard day's work.

Bed and Bored

A silver-haired woman shared with me the promise she made to her husband on their wedding day: "I cannot promise you continuous ecstasy or hell, but I do promise you this—you will never be bored!"

I believe a man can stand almost anything but boredom. A group of husbands who had been unfaithful to their wives were interviewed as to why they had wandered. The overwhelming reason was boredom. Eighty percent said they were just plain bored at home and wanted a "new experience."

Every man needs excitement and high adventure at his own address. After all, the same nightie worn night after night and month after month loses some of its sex appeal with each passing year.

Husbands sometimes tire of nighties anyway, so why not try some outlandish "costume" which is far less expensive and far more fun. Across the land husbands have responded like gangbusters as their wives met them at the door in some shocking outfit.

What is a "costume"? It is anything different from

what you usually wear. A young wife who always wore jeans and sneakers from morning till night greeted her hubby in a skirt and low-cut blouse. He asked, "Is this my Christmas present early?" Later he admitted to her that when he came home at night he never knew whether she was "going to or coming from the gym."

Husbands love the excitement of a costume. The shock value brings several side benefits: First of all, it sets the scene for romance and lets him know you care about meeting his needs.

Second, he's suddenly eager to meet yours. A wife looking spicy helps increase a man's "caring" ability. A man has to get past the visual barrier of how a woman looks before he can care how she feels.

Third, in dressing up for him, you also can't help but feel a little excited and lighthearted too. When you're acting like a kid, your barriers are down and that's good for sex.

Finally, if he knows you might surprise him some night, he will never bring home unexpected company for dinner without calling first!

Some women have reacted negatively to the suggestion of "dressing up" for their husbands. In one Total Woman seminar a lady blurted out, "This is utter nonsense! My husband doesn't care about all those silly things. We're more adult than that."

Two months later, the woman called her class instructor, but now she was very contrite. "I had to call you," she said, as she began to sob. "Last night my husband asked for a divorce. He said I had always acted like his mother. I always put the children first and never had time for him or sex. The things you talked about in class are the very things he said I didn't do. It's too late for us now, but please tell the other women I was wrong."

Another woman, who had been married for twenty-one years, was also dubious about dressing up for hubby. She said she just couldn't visualize doing some of the costume things, "but my husband thinks otherwise."

One young man who "thought otherwise" wrote earnestly, "My wife and I see very little of each other since we both work. When I get home at midnight, she is sound asleep. I don't expect her to wait up every night, but it would be nice if she surprised me once in a while. Say, for example, I walk in the door and there she is, all decked out. . . ."

A prominent doctor made a list for his wife of six things he desired most upon his arrival home each night:

1. Have house presentable.
2. Be attired in a negligee.
3. Provide twenty minutes for me to relax before being presented with the crises of the day.
4. Be attired in a negligee.
5. Have meal ready within an hour.
6. Be attired in a negligee.

Note: If negligee is black, items 1, 3, & 5 may be omitted.

Candid Costume

For one wife, even the thought of buying a frilly nightie caused all sorts of consternation. She felt silly and embarassed. Finally her practical nature triumphed and she purchased some red, white, and blue Bicentennial pajamas. Her husband wasn't sure whether he should kiss her or salute. She added, "But we really enjoyed playing 'Capture the Flag.' "

I recall a dear grandmother (the buxom, earthy type) who attended a class. When she heard her costume assignment, she chuckled and blurted out in a robust voice, "Oh, this'll kill Pop."

The next week I watched for her since I was rather concerned about Pop's health. I saw her come jostling into class, eyes flashing with excitement. She hurried over to me, laughing heartily. "We had the best week ever, Honey. Pop never had himself such a time!"

A blind lady attended one of the classes. Although her husband was also blind, they had two children with perfect eyesight. This lady was determined to do all the assignments and the first week, for her extra special dinner assignment, she baked a sweet potato souffle and stuck a candle in it.

As she was donning her "costume" of lots of jewelry and a long dress, her preteen children came into her bedroom. When they realized she was "dressing up" so elegantly for daddy, they rushed into the living room, shouting exuberantly, "Daddy, Daddy, come feel Mommy!"

Whether six years or twenty-six years have rolled by, you can bring your marriage back to life. Meet boredom head-on.

After twenty years of married life which had plateaued years ago and was on a downward tilt, Bob longed for a surprise. In the words of country singer Loretta Lynn, "the tingle had become a chill." No sex, no communication, but "lots of nagging about smoking and weight and staying away on business trips." Bob only smoked more but enjoyed it less.

One night he told his wife, Helen, "I love you, but I can't live with you. I can't stand this constant tension."

That was the turning point for her. She determined to change *Helen,* to appreciate him instead of putting him down, and to accept him instead of trying to correct his faults.

Soon he was able to see the change in her attitude, and slowly he began to talk. Helen wrote, "The little pats on the fanny returned and we began to really have some 'super sex' with the help of my own costumes and a variety of rooms in which to party. (Beanbag chairs are one of my favorite places.) Please pass on what I have discovered, not just to the young ones with the seven-year itch, but to the now-growing group with the twenty-year itch!"

Just as important as your appearance is the place you choose to share your love. Scenes of costumes and subsequent times of "beautiful loving" have been reported from the most interesting locations—diving boards, trampolines, bales of hay, sleeping bags—anyplace just so long as it takes perfunctory intercourse out of the category of "boring."

Perhaps you can't have a costume party once a week, but how about once a month? How about once a year?

Maybe just once in a lifetime? Sometime, somewhere, when he least expects it. . . .

Reports of hundreds of different costumes have flooded in from around the country. They prove that American women are extremely creative. One woman confessed modestly that her costume was such a show-stopper, even her poodle barked. Instead of hoarding these ideas, I wanted to share some with you. So here's to new vistas!

The Turkish Exchange.   "After 11 years of law school, starting law practice, two little boys, and the daily grind," the Chicago wife wrote, "we were in the 'downhill slide.' By the time my boys are in bed every night and our Turkish exchange student is practicing the harp and listening to his English records, my husband has long since taken his briefcase to the basement to work, and I'm all alone upstairs."

On Monday she determined to turn things around. She went to the discount store and bought a whole sackful of inexpensive bedroom costumes. That night she put on the first outfit, and on the intercom called her husband, Arnold, who was in the basement. He rushed upstairs, took one look at her and asked, "Have you been drinking?" Then he turned around and went back down to the basement.

She was crushed but determined to try again.

On Tuesday night, after everyone else was in bed, she served Arnold supper in the bedroom with flowers, mild incense, "Bolero" on the stereo, with her in lace bikinis and black net stockings. "Arnold's eyes nearly fell out of his head. We never did get to the coffee and cake," she wrote. "He plans to take me on a second honeymoon. I know there are lots of other things I have to work on, but at least I have his attention now. The rest will come."

Saint Pat's Parade.   "The idea of costumes sounds like fun," a woman wrote, "but with a limited wardrobe, I just can't seem to come up with any ideas. How can I accomplish costuming on a budget so short my children are on a free-lunch program at school?"

It doesn't take extra money or time to make life exciting, just a little imagination and the desire. A simple bed sheet for example can be an effective wraparound.

Jana wrapped a baby-blue sheet around her, toga-style, and reclined on the chaise with a platter of grapes. She ate all the grapes while she waited for Fred! When he *finally* arrived, she demurely lifted the sheet corner and smiled, "I wanted to help you unwind. Start here." The next morning her husband, relaxed and unwound, beamed, "Honey, last night is a memory of you that I'll never forget."

An Irish colleen celebrated Saint Patrick's Day by filling tarts with green vanilla pudding for dessert. Her little girl helped make hats for their Royal Leprechaun family—king, queen, and princess of Shamrock Land. "I can hardly wait to see Bill's reaction to green mashed potatoes," she said. "And I wonder whether green Magic Marker shamrocks will wipe off certain body areas easily."

Tea for Two.   It's great fun to use whatever is available around the house to create a costume. The simplest items can be the most effective. Women have reported (with success) the use of old hats, old clothing altered, and shaving cream—even stick-on bows and tea bags for tassels!

A Michigan housewife scoured her house for available "atmosphere" items. She put a psychedelic light bulb in the bedroom lamp and twisted some rolls of red crepe paper into streamers from ceiling to bed frame on three sides around the bed. Instead of tape, she used a package of Stickum, a gumlike substance, to hold up the streamers. Digging through boxes, she found a square of fake fur which she draped over the middle section of her sofa cushion, and propped this on the bed with a few stuffed pillows. She brought in a red potted geranium from the front porch—the only fresh flowers she could find. A few candles, cologne, and a flimsy red nightie finished the total picture.

Her husband worked nights so she anxiously awaited his return at midnight. "His reaction," she wrote, "was utter surprise and the evening was a delight. I write this to ask one question: How do you remove twelve green spots of Stickum from a white ceiling?"

"Trick or Treat."   Three years ago while my friends Stephanie Noonan and Sara Slaton and I were guests on the Phil Donahue Show in Green Bay, Wisconsin, Stephanie gave a suggestion for the approaching Halloween season. "Wait until after all the little trick-or-treaters are gone, then take off your clothes and put on a mask, a wig, and a trench coat. Slip out the back door, come around

to the front and ring the doorbell. When your husband opens the front door, fling open your trench coat and sing out, "Trick or treat!"

That Halloween night husbands everywhere were met by an apparition at the front door, clothed only in a coat, mask, and wig. A number of reports have filtered in.

In California after the steady stream of tiny goblins subsided, the mother of the house finally donned her costume, and rang the doorbell. When her weary husband opened the front door, he saw Frankenstein with a blond wig and boots. Suddenly she flung open her coat, flashed her costume, and shouted, "Trick or treat!" He was dazed, but recovered quickly. Then with obvious perception and delight, he grinned, "My, you're an *old* one, aren't you?"

In Oklahoma, an older woman put on her teenager's gorilla head and raincoat, and sneaked outside. Fearful of what her neighbors might see, she knocked on the *back* door. When her unsuspecting husband answered the knock, she shyly opened her coat. He was so startled at the bizarre trick-or-treater that he involuntarily stepped back and fell down the basement steps, breaking his leg.

A woman from Ohio wrote, "I thought the Halloween thing was so cute, I'm going to try it myself—pregnant or not. On second thought, maybe I'll add some orange crepe paper and be the Great Pumpkin." Not only children have happy memories of Halloween, nowadays.

Dick West, UPI columnist, gave some advice to *hus-*

bands to surprise their wives. A well-prepared husband should keep a suitcase full of costumes in the trunk of his car. "As you are driving home from work," he wrote, "stop at a gas station, go into the men's room and change into one of these outfits. One evening you might arrive home dressed as an apartment doorman. The next evening you might be a scuba diver, a brain surgeon, a bank robber, or the ticket-taker in a dime-a-dance parlor. The important thing is to keep your wife in suspense."

The Missionary Position.   Amorous, adventurous wives everywhere are spicing up their marriage bed to the ecstatic joy of husbands. A poignant letter came from a young missionary in Africa.

She and her family lived in a remote area with only the barest necessities of life. She told how she had searched for nighties at the open-air market. "Of course they're just filthy, torn, and picked over by the time they get this far. But I did find one little orange number, just my size, so my undies stock is somewhat replenished."

My heart went out to her. I imagined how I would feel in her circumstances on the other side of the world, so I decided to send her a few fluffy, feathery things that might make the African nights more exotic. Actually, when I folded all the items together, the whole lot was too small for a package so I tucked them in a manila envelope and mailed them off to her.

In a month or so an airmail letter arrived, postmarked AFRICA. I eagerly tore it open and began to read.

"Dear Marabel . . . dear, *dear* Marabel . . . dear, dear, dear!!!

"The envelope came yesterday!! The size of it immediately gripped my curiosity. I ran to the bedroom at the back of the house, locked the doors, and ripped it open. I'm glad they came in a plain brown wrapper!!! . . . .

("Make six more lines of dots mentally!)

"My husband came to the door and wondered why it was locked at 11:00 A.M. 'Hey, Hon,' he called, 'What's the matter?' I replied, 'They've come!' "

Needless to say, her husband was floored. "We nearly died laughing over the feathers . . ." she wrote me, "and then we stopped laughing. . . ."

Foggy Fred.   With two small children around the house, it was most difficult for Dorothy to be creative and yet discreet. "After dinner I gently whispered in my husband's ear, 'I may not look very sexy on the outside, but underneath I am totally bare.'

"If it hadn't been for the children," she said, "I do believe he would have thrown me down right there on the dining room floor and attacked me. Instead, we put the kids to bed very early and the rest was wonderful, totally fulfilled beyond words."

And what if your husband doesn't respond to your surprise? First of all, check to see if your attitude matches your costume. My friend Gail Larson said, "Your attitude is the most important costume you can wear, and also the least expensive, but sometimes the hardest to change."

Your husband may think you have wrecked the car, so if he reacts like Dubious Dan or Cyril Cynic, don't be surprised. If he looks like Stunned Stan, give him time to revive. And finally, if there's no reaction at all, take his pulse!

A visiting relative once explained to Archie Bunker that marriage after twenty-five years is like opening a Cracker Jack box with no surprise inside. TV hubby Archie reacted, "What's wrong with just the Cracker Jacks?"

Nothing at all, Archie. Whatever turns you on. But lots of other men love a surprise.

If your husband doesn't like costumes or anything else I recommend, or anything anyone else recommends for that matter, for goodness sakes, don't do it! The whole point is to please *him* and meet his needs. This is a positive step toward meeting your own.

First Timers

Orgasm or the lack of one, rates high among a woman's sex problems. Since the subject of orgasm is such a private topic anyway, that makes it difficult for many women to discuss it. Some have even written to ask, "How can my *friend* get an orgasm?"

A woman confided that her husband's biggest disappointment is that she doesn't reach an orgasm—"almost but not quite." Her husband feels great pleasure himself, but thinks he is cheating her.

Of course, the goal of sexual intercourse is not the orgasm itself, but rather the closeness, the oneness, and the mutual love. If, however, orgasm can be reached, it satisfies the woman in so many ways.

Volumes have been written on the single subject of orgasm, some as dry and lifeless as the shelves on which they rest. Whatever the dynamics, Dr. David Reuben says, "The only thing that stands between any woman and an unlimited number of orgasmic experiences is about two pounds of tissue—the brain." Only your brain can tell yourself, "It's okay—just relax and enjoy." As you surrender (so to speak), you will reach the threshold of the climax, and one day you will go over the peak into the intense thrill and exquisite relief of the orgasm.

A housewife, married twenty-five years with five kids wrote, "As much as I have tried to relax, I have never had an orgasm. My husband doesn't know where the clitoris is."

"Tell him," I told her. If *your* husband is also in the dark on this matter, tell him where your clitoris is, and anything else that you particularly like to have caressed. You will probably reach a beautiful orgasm when he gently and patiently applies a rhythmic pressure to your clitoris. But knowing its location is essential! Don't give up. It may take time, but it's worth the wait.

After five years of marriage Sandy decided that love-making with her husband would be beautiful love, not just sex. "After all," she said, "if God had all those good intentions for us, who was I to challenge them? I have had my first climax ever! My husband is so thrilled and I've been smiling ever since."

Standing Ovation

Sex renews and restores a man. All over the country women are discovering, some for the first time, that sex recharges them too. Other theraputic benefits have been reported by both men and women that "sex beats aspirin," relieves tension, and can even help in weight control.

After a session of supersex, men often become very creative. One satisfied fellow turned the tables and surprised his wife, after they had made love early one evening. When she came home from a meeting late that night, she discovered her entire ironing hanging neatly all over the family room, and propped up on the ironing board was a large sign: I LOVE YOU, TOTAL WOMAN!

A change of attitude changes all sorts of things. An artist's wife began to meet her husband's needs in every way she could. And once she began, did he ever change! "He adores painting," she said, "but when I say I'm ready for bed, he drops his brushes and runs. He even switched from oils to acrylics to clean up faster!"

Psychologists say that every man has two needs which, if met by his wife, will cause him to absolutely adore her. One is warm sexual love, and the other: compliments.

When George came home from work one evening, Ann knew he was drained and drawn. He needed a sudden and desperate dose of both sex and compliments. Following a delicious dinner, creative Ann retired to the bedroom, determined to satisfy those two important needs. After they made mad, passionate love that night, Ann leaped out of bed and applauded!

R. WILLEMAN

Assignment

1. Paint your bedroom. Choose a soft color you love, buy a roller, and whip it on the walls yourself. Paint the trim, woodwork, and ceilings pure white. If your room is beautiful, you will be likely to tackle whatever the day or night might bring.

2. Set the mood for love at breakfast (if he has one!). Use candlelight at the table, especially in the winter, or if it's still dark outside. On the weekend, or when there is no rush for work, serve him breakfast in bed. While he's still asleep, bring in coffee, sweet rolls, and orange juice on a tray set with your best dishes. Slip into something sexy and then waken him with a kiss.

3. Set the bedroom mood for love. Buy some tinted light bulbs for special bedroom occasions, or drape a

red nightie over the lamp shade to give a diffused, warm, soft glow. Begin now to anticipate making love tonight. Be available and touchable, but not overly aggressive.

Part Four
The Joy of Living

9 *Peace Talks*

From the first day I met Charlie until the day of our marriage, we never experienced one moment of tension in our conversation. We talked nonstop on any and every subject. I never felt uneasy around him. I was enthralled over this most interesting and talkative man. One evening I remember sitting for hours locked in discussion in a cozy corner booth. Only when the waiter's icy stares penetrated our peaceful realm did we return to the world of reality.

I knew that married life with Charlie would always be just as exciting and stimulating. My world was vibrant, the stars shone brightly, and the grass seemed one shade greener. My heart sang with the birds each morning. How I loved this talkative guy.

And then we got married!

You may have seen the cartoon of a man sitting at the breakfast table reading his paper. His wife is sure he's not listening but she asks, "Are you listening to me?"

"Of course, dear," he replies.

Frustrated, she shouts, "You know, the baby has jungle rot!"

"Yes, dear," he replies.

"The County Inspector condemned our house because it's being eaten by giant termites."

"Yes, dear," he replies.

"The Communists have bombed New York and shot the President!"

"Yes, dear," he replies.

Exasperated, she slams her coffee cup down and stalks out. Hubby peers over his paper, shakes his head, and thinks to himself, "Who in the world can understand women?"

Happy Talk

"The trouble with most marriages today," according to one marriage counselor, "is that Mr. and Mrs. America cannot communicate with each other."

Communication is verbal intercourse using words to exchange messages or opinions. Throughout our first year of marriage, the barriers slowly began to build. I didn't know what made them come, and I didn't know how to make them go away. Eventually our communication broke down. So did our sex life. Though we tried to make up after a quarrel, I never felt our breach was fully healed.

Before I could speak what was really in my heart, I needed a climate of receptivity, and so did Charlie. I didn't know that a man cannot communicate with a nagging wife. *I* was making Charlie's love for me dry up. I was the one who was cutting off communication. I was ignorant of knowing how to meet his needs. When I discovered how, Charlie began to talk again.

In any marriage—or any other relationship—when the lines of communication are open with give and take on *both* sides, there is usually hope for settling almost any kind of problem. How do you keep these lines open? May I offer a few suggestions that have worked for others and for me?

Think on These Things.   Since I tend to speak before I think, I try to follow a general rule taken from the Bible: "Fix your thoughts on what is true and good and right. Think about things that are pure and lovely, and dwell on the fine, good things in others. Think about all you can praise God for and be glad about."[16]

I realize this admonition sounds slightly Pollyanna, but following it miraculously brings joy to my heart. Hatred, jealousy, bitterness, and fear are negative and devastating emotions. When I deliberately think "on the good," I begin to feel kindly toward Charlie—and other people too—and I am not nearly as likely to tear them down.

"People don't care how much you know," said Carlton Booth, "until they know how much you care."

Point 1. Think about the positive qualities in others.

Engine Blocks.   "What should I do?" the letter began. "When I was a stupid, young kid, I married a man
twenty-six years older than I. Now I go one way and he
goes the other, and neither of us can carry on a conversation about anything. Can this marriage, or my nerves, or
health, or peace of mind be helped in any way?"

Because of the age difference, the circumstances in
this case were difficult but not impossible. To break the
silence in any generation, I find it's always helpful to talk
about the interests of the other person.

The wife of an amateur racer wrote, "I almost caused
a car wreck while my husband and I were discussing his
rebuilt Vega. I suggested he put in a small engine block
for the holiday race. Steve slammed on the brakes (forgetting the car behind us), and with the most pleased
expression asked, 'Where did you learn that?' His profes-
sion is in automotive technology, so I guess I learned it
from him. He loved it!"

Point 2. Talk about his interests.

Questions and Answers.   Whenever I am stumped
for a conversation opener with my husband or anyone
else, I find that a question is the answer. However egotis-
tical it may seem, nevertheless each of us is delighted
when another person really cares, and asks questions
about our interests in life.

When I am asked a civil question, I think, "My, isn't
that person interesting?" When I'm answering questions
on familiar ground, there is no strain at all and I become

animated with the details of my own life.

I find that questions designed to "draw out" the other person also help put him at ease. These questions not only stimulate conversation and create an immediate rapport, but I also learn from what's being said. When I speak, I know what I'm going to say, but I don't know what someone else might say.

Dorothy Shula, wife of the Miami Dolphins' head coach told me, "When Don is a guest speaker, he is usually seated at the head table with distinguished people. He makes it a point to ask about their specialties, and always comes away having learned from them."

Albert Einstein said that asking questions was also a prime source of input for him. He never stopped asking those "childlike questions." Remember, the more questions a woman asks, the more she learns, and the more she learns the better her decisions.

Point 3. Ask questions.

Nonstop Express.   Some years ago, Charlie and I were invited to the opening of an art center. Amid the milling and the introductions, I was fascinated by the arrival of one rather boisterous woman. I watched as she circled the large room introducing herself. After a few brief, trite comments she looked around beyond her immediate circle, like a periscope scanning the seas 180 degrees.

She moved toward us and insisted we met before "somewhere." We received the same "polite trite" and then I was aware of her eyes looking past me. Up periscope. Swivel. Another prey spotted. And off she went.

It was all so sudden. I knew that the self-proclaimed Ms. Wonderful had probably intended to leave us in a cloud of awe, yet not once had she asked us a question. In fact, she never even took the time to learn our names.

I continued to watch as she talked nonstop to other people who were not responding to her. I wondered why she acted that way. Perhaps beneath her exterior of apparent confidence, she felt a sense of insecurity.

The Duchess of Windsor once said, "A woman must learn to be a good listener." I agree. Not because she is a woman, but because listening doesn't come naturally for anyone. We all come into this world wanting the world to listen to us. Children often outshout each other to be heard, and that includes children of all ages.

Nonstop talkers usually need reassuring, but my impulse is to avoid them. Any husband married to one usually feels the same way.

Kathy the Chatterbox never understood what caused her divorce—until it was too late. "No wonder he is now in the arms of my best friend," she grieved. She admitted how negative she had been. "I nagged, whined, and treated him like a naughty little boy, talking down at him, and thwarting every aspiration. Of course, if anyone had asked me last month about this mess, I would have cried and said it was all Larry's fault."

With much regret she continued, "I simply was forcing him to go out and do what he did. I realize now he has been very lonesome and unhappy for years. If only I had seen it then. I thought our communication was good, but how could it have been if *he* never had a chance to say a word!"

Point 4. Stop, look and listen.

Word of Discouragement.   I watched a televised golf
match recently as Jack Nicklaus and another golfer were
preparing to putt. Jack's playing partner went first. He
carefully lined up the putt and hit it. It looked good, but
then it just slid by the hole. The commentator said,
"He'll never win playing like that."

Then it was Jack's turn. His was a shorter putt and he
took longer to line it up. Plunk, he hit it. The ball rolled
six inches past the hole. This time the commentator
remarked, "That's *most unusual* to see Jack miss one like
that."

What a difference in comments: "He'll never win"
versus "That's most unusual." Same shots and same commentator and same scores, yet one remark was discouraging, the other encouraging.

Abraham Lincoln said, "You cannot help small men by
tearing down big men. You cannot strengthen the weak
by weakening the strong."

Wives and commentators alike are often guilty of "the
discouraging word." One Saturday Dave decided to trim
some enormous trees that overpowered his backyard.
He worked all day and at 4 o'clock his wife, who had
been shopping, came home just as Dave was wiping his
face on his sleeve. "Well," he said wearily, "how's it
look?"

She dismissed all his backbreaking work with a glance,
and emphatically stated, "You sure have a long way to
go!"

What a master at the subtle put-down. She could have

helped soothe Dave's fatigue simply by saying, "Honey, you're doing a great job! I know it's hot out here, but look how much you have cleared out. This yard is going to be beautiful!"

In so many American houses there seldom is heard an encouraging word, and the clouds are just stormy all day.

Point 5. Encourage.

When I Hurt

For me, the most difficult time to communicate is when I am hurt. Not the Band-Aid and aspirin hurt, but the hurt hurt. The mad hurt. The disillusioned hurt. When that happens it's impossible for me to keep cool, and that's bad if you're married to a calm lawyer, who may be snoozing while home burns.

I have been this route a number of times, and I'm glad to pass on some simple tips from personal experience (and from other women) on how to ride through the fire.

Don't Slam the Door.   Whenever I am mad or under pressure, I have a tendency to react immediately and negatively to any new idea. And when I say *no!*—in my mind I slam the door, inevitably on Charlie.

Door-slamming, either in reality or in my mind, causes an ultimatum—a do-it-or-else situation. Door-slamming is dangerous because all communication is cut off. It leaves no further room whatsoever for negotiation or compromise. Nor does it allow the other person to save face, be it my husband, my neighbor, or my friend. So rather than making a sudden, drastic decision, I try to give myself time to think and cool off.

Don't Clam Up.   The Bible says if you are angry, ". . . don't sin by nursing your grudge. Don't let the sun go down with you still angry—get over it quickly. . . . Instead, be kind to each other, tenderhearted, forgiving one another, just as God has forgiven you. . . ."[17]

I heard a husband joke about his marriage, "My wife and I never go to bed angry, but once we stayed up for three months!" Problems which aren't resolved before going to bed loom so much larger the next day, and if they continue unsettled, may begin to affect your health.

Syndicated columnist Dr. T.R. Van Dellen wrote, "Healthy and vigorous men usually can take ordinary aches and pains in stride, but anger, frustration, and gloom sap their strength. For centuries, emotional upsets such as anger have been known to bring chest pains (angina pectoris) and sudden death. Hostility elevates the blood pressure, constricts blood vessels, increases gastric acidity, churns up the stomach, and raises the blood sugar."

At times, a woman leaves arguments unresolved and allows bitterness to build simply because she fears a confrontation. It is no fun for anyone to stand eyeball-to-eyeball with a pounding heartbeat and a lump in the throat, defending a position, but because confrontations jolt people into thinking and taking a stand, they are sometimes necessary.

One proverb says, "A wise man restrains his anger and

overlooks insults. This is to his credit."[18] If you are secure within yourself, you can pass over many minor irritations, but you may find you can't restrain and overlook major ones. If you carry on an imaginary confrontation in your mind day after day, your imaginary opponent will soon become your master and rob you of life. Rather than be his frustrated slave, it's far better to express your feelings verbally and peaceably, if possible.

If something is gnawing away inside you, don't clam up. But when you speak, be careful to attack the problem and not the person. You need not compromise your stand, but your kindness may persuade where words would not. Remember that "a man persuaded against his will is of the same opinion still."

Don't Duck the Blame.   When your husband knows you have accepted him totally, sometimes he will start telling you what he doesn't like. This too is communication. If he feels free to tell you, how great. Respond by listening. While he is talking, don't interrupt to defend yourself. And if you see that you were wrong or that his way might be better, admit it. How difficult to say those three simple words, "I was wrong."

Don't Carry Chips.   Once the war is over, then forgive him and forget it. The very word *forgive* implies that you've been wronged, and is not conditioned on someone else apologizing first. Forgiveness may even be a one-way street. For Jesus it was.

He said to *keep on* forgiving—490 times. Maybe that refers to the repeated angry emotion which keeps popping up every time you remember your raw deal. Anger, with instant replay, requires repeated doses of forgiveness.

When He Hurts

Early in our marriage, Charlie explained to me the meaning of "lawyer-client privilege." Simply stated, that meant because of his confidential relationship with his clients, he couldn't tell me about their problems. He couldn't even tell me *who* came in the office. I felt a little hurt but tried to understand.

One night he shared with me a little tidbit about a case without mentioning names. I was excited (drunk with power, actually) over my *in* knowledge and the next night I blurted it out to a group of friends. Charlie looked horror-stricken. I suddenly realized that our guests must be the clients he had talked about!

That was the start of our communication breakdown. I had betrayed his confidence, and he knew he couldn't trust me. Many years went by before he dared trust ol' Loudmouth again. Of course, he still never talks about *who* or *what* from the law office, but we do confide in each other in all other areas.

A Detroit housewife wrote, "My friends and I discuss our husband's faults and then sigh over how nice it would be if they'd just 'come around.' " Loyalty is a quality that is essential for any relationship and especially a marriage. Loyalty means being faithful and true and constant. Disloyalty is tearing down. While it's important for a wife not to nag her husband and not to keep her opinions bottled up inside, it's equally important that she not be a Traitor Vickie.

Proverbs states, "He [or she] who covers and forgives an offense seeks love, but he [or she] who repeats or harps on a matter separates even close friends."[19] And marriages.

Singing superstar Wayne Newton recently referred to his wife, Elaine, as "the total show-business wife." He said, "When she comes to see my show, it's as a fan, for which I'm thankful. Sure don't need her telling me what to do and what not to do. Got enough critics already."

In some circles, being your husband's critic is a popular pastime. Dr. Thomas Harris, author of *I'm OK— You're OK*, writes, "Someone who is enjoying the game of 'Ain't it Awful' does not welcome the intrusion of facts. If the neighbor girls enjoy an every-morning session of 'Husbands Are Stupid,' they will not welcome the new girl who announces brightly that her husband is a jewel."

Chapter Thirteen of 1 Corinthians is known as "the Love Chapter" in the Bible. If you love someone, verse seven states that you will be loyal to him, "no matter what the cost." Loyalty is then defined in at least three ways:[20]

1. *Always believe in him.* When you and your husband have a disagreement, you can be for the *man* even though you may not be for the plan.
2. *Always expect the best of him.* When your husband

suggests a new idea, encourage him. Instead of expecting the worst by nagging him and dragging your heels,
be his #1 cheerleader. Tell him you know he can do it,
and watch the *esprit de corps* of your family rise.

3. *Always stand your ground in defending him.* Many
wives are working on a PhD degree in Putting Hubby
Down. This favorite course is designed to destroy all
confidence and initiative in your man. Putting hubby
down is also putting yourself down. After all, he is *your*
husband.

Breaking the Silence

Several years ago, a questionnaire was circulated
among military enlisted men asking what one require-
ment they most sought in a wife. Surprisingly (to me,
anyway), their number one desire—above beauty, sex, or
intellect—was comfort.

A man comes home to be comforted and comfortable.
If your man has had "one of those days," his comfort
level is probably way down. You can help bring the level
back up until it registers: *Confident Again.*

These principles of communication deal with all inter-
personal relationships. They have restored "Happy
Talk." They have eased the pain when she hurts and
when he hurts. Thousands have written to say they do
work.

10 All in the Family

A lonely, love-starved teenager wrote, "I was born with a pervasive melancholy. What frustrated me most was that I had no ties to family or friends. There was nothing of lasting worth and value. I led a detached existence and I was a parody of a person—literally and figuratively. I didn't tell jokes. I *was* a joke.

"I stopped growing long ago," he continued. "I never did develop into a real person, and I cannot tolerate the false and empty existence I have created. I am no longer interested in this world—and know it is not interested in me."

On Valentine's Day 1975, a couple driving through the woods in Louisiana found his body hanging from the limb of a tree, a bed sheet tied around his neck.

A jarful of notepaper lay against the tree trunk. One

scrap read, "If you pursue who I was and spend hundreds of dollars, you will accomplish little. There are no legal consequences of my death, or any kind of entanglements. All that can happen is that you will shatter the domestic peace and order of two innocent lives. Do not deprive them of the hope that their 'missing son' will return. Let me be. Let it be as if I wasn't ever here. Simply cremate me as 'John Doe.' "

At last report the body was buried unidentified and unclaimed.

Hot Potato

The story is told that once President James Garfield and a friend were crossing the street when suddenly Garfield bowed to the little newsboy on the corner. As they continued on, the President's friend asked him, "Did you know him?"

"No," answered Garfield, "but I bowed because no one knows *who* is buttoned inside that boy's jacket."

A boy is the only thing that God can use to make a man. In His process of "making a man," what an important part parents play—especially the mother. Traditionally, mothers spend more time with their children during the formative years. Even though a mother may accept the challenge resolutely and even eagerly, at times the weight of this responsibility seems overwhelming.

When one of those "overwhelming days" hits, a mother's first tendency is to blame the little screaming banshee for being incorrigible and irresponsible. The kid is the culprit. Or is he? If parents hardly know how to raise their children, how can you expect a child to lead the way?

Many authors have compared children to plants. They both need nurturing, watering, and weeding. Isn't it interesting today that gardeners talk to their plants, and even play music to make them grow? If horticulturists talk to their plants, how about trying it with your kids?

Give your child your time—lots of it—for soon he'll be gone and your time of influence gone. It takes time to cultivate a climate in which children can grow strong and healthy.

After Junior and the baby have whined and screamed all day, it is a mother's natural tendency not only to blame the kids, but also her husband. I used to nag Charlie from the minute he walked in the door, "Please! Play with your kids. They don't even know they have a father. I've had them all day. Here, you take them!" To him, it was like changing of the guards. No wonder he only pulled the newspaper higher.

But when I began to meet Charlie's needs as a person, he became a wonderful husband and father. He acted as if he were seeing the girls for the first time, and began to spend hours playing with them.

I see now that the best way to help a child is to help his parents, starting with Mom. If parents don't like what their child has done, it's not the child alone who must change. As one marriage counselor said, "If Johnny is a hot potato, he is not going to cool off by being thrown from expert to expert, unless something is done about the oven at home." In fixing the oven, I believe that one of the best things a mother can do for her children is to love their daddy.

Something Better

A mother's influence helps determine whether her children will be either burdens or blessings. When I mentioned this in a seminar, one woman leaned over to her friend and whispered, "I have one of each!"

The task of child-raising is awesome and difficult, yet paradoxically it is also easy and fun. The principles are so simple, we sophisticated twentieth-century earthlings often miss them. Unfortunately, the littlest earthlings do too.

Henry Anslinger, former director of the U.S. Bureau of Narcotics said, "Many factors are contributing to the mental and moral failure of our young people, the most important of which is the failure of the home itself."

"Close family ties, warmth, and love represent the true alternative to drugs," says Dr. Joel Fort of Fort Help in San Francisco, "—the something positive that shows a child that pleasure and meaning in life come from the inside out, not the outside in."

When a doctor asked a young addict why he used drugs, the addict countered, "Why not?" The doctor pursued, "How could someone convince you to stop?"

"Show me something better," he answered.

That's our goal. All day long Charlie and I talk and

pray and work to give our children "something better."
Here's a glimpse of some of the principles by which we
live.

In the Morning

A mother told me she no longer kissed her daughter
because she figured a teenager "outgrew that sort of
thing." Once she realized the importance of physical
contact, she began to kiss her daughter good-bye in the
mornings as she left for school.

The mother later reported on her project. "When I
kissed her the first morning, she pulled away and said,
'Oh, Mom!' The second morning she didn't pull away,
but she didn't respond much either. The third morning
she kissed *me!"*

Hug and Hold.   No matter how old your child is, it's
never too late to start. All across America, thousands of
people meet daily in therapy groups with the main purpose of contacting and touching one another. Every person is born with a basic human need to be touched by
others. Parents who withhold that touch are not meeting
this vital need and are depriving their children of the
security of feeling loved.

A child who does not receive the stroking he needs
may go looking for it. Psychologists urge parents to keep
on hugging and roughhousing with their kids, especially
as they come into their teen years. They say the reason
for rampant teenage-sex may not be that kids so much

want to have intercourse, but that they just need to be held.

Touching may also make a child receptive to learning skills. A grade-school teacher said she had tried everything in the book to teach one of her students to read, but to no avail. Finally, she took the six-year-old in her arms and held him in her lap, as they sounded out the words together. He learned to read in no time at all!

Henry Ward Beecher said, "The first hour of the morning is the rudder of the day," so each morning when I wake up I kiss my girls enthusiastically. One day last week I missed. I awoke exhausted and trudged my way to the kitchen. In a few minutes Michelle padded in and watched me making breakfast in my foggy state. After a few minutes of being ignored, she sighed mournfully, "No one's kissed me all morning." We had only been up five minutes, but already she was thinking, *Something's missing.*

Boys need a mother's touch just as girls do. Marian's fourteen-year-old son, who is six feet tall, usually shrugs when she hugs. "But if he goes to bed before I do," she said, "he'll come and kind of stand around and say, 'Well, I'm going to bed now . . . ' He knows I'll kiss him and tell him I love him. Even though he's a boy-man, he still needs that touch."

Love Unconditionally.   Mr. Carlson's son was arrested on a drug charge. The next day Mr. Carlson told the incident to his associate, who remarked, "If he were my son, I'd kick him out!"

"If he were your son, I'd kick him out, too!" Carlson shot back. "But he's not; he's mine."

My girls know that I'll never kick them out—no matter what. Of course, I don't always condone everything they do, but that doesn't affect my relationship with them. They know I will always love them, even though I may be against their actions, and hopefully, this will provide an anchor for them throughout the teenage years. I say "hopefully" since Laura and Michelle aren't teenagers yet, so I can't give tried and proven personal examples, only what others have shared.

My friend Lynn explained to her seven-year-old daughter she too would always love her unconditionally, no matter what. A month later, Lynn was late for a meeting and shoved dinner at her family. Then she ran frantically out the door, snarling at her youngster, who tried to kiss her good-bye.

While driving to the meeting, Lynn felt immersed in guilt at her own inexcusable behavior. She stopped at a pay phone to call home. When her little girl answered, Lynn began, "Honey, please forgive me for the way I acted at dinner. I was pressed for time, but that's no excuse and I'm so sorry."

"Oh, Mommy," the little girl said sweetly, "you didn't have to call. You know I love you *unconditionally.*"

This mother had done her homework and though she had become "fragmented" temporarily, the solid principles of unconditional love had been instilled in her family and they "held" in times of stress.

Encourage.   A child's feeling of worth is transmitted from his parents by various means, among them the acts of hugging, accepting, loving, and encouraging. Praise especially does wonders for a child in helping to develop his or her own special abilities. Studies have shown that children who are praised perform much better on skill tests than do children who are not.

Psychologist Henry Brandt encourages parents to have "confident expectation." If a mother believes in what she is doing for her children, she will confidently expect the child to cooperate. Here again, attitude is all-important. If she expects the best, her child will want to give his best. Not perfection, just his best. Expecting perfection wipes out a child's ability to succeed, as witnessed by many frustrated sons, who try in vain to live up to their father's unattainable standards.

I heard of a family where all three sons are athletes. Whenever one of the boys plays in a game and his team loses, he is not permitted to eat dinner with the rest of the family that night. His parents and brothers tell him, "We don't eat with losers!"

Can you imagine what this does to his self-esteem? On the other hand, the mother who tells her son, "You can do it! I know you can!" sends a confident youngster to school or play. If he fails in the process he knows he is still loved. He also has a freedom to fail. But if Mom believes in him, he dares to believe in himself, and that's a giant step for a little guy.

In the Afternoon

Two years ago, I decided to drop the car pool and pick up my children myself after school. I realize that not every mother can do this, but in my case I arranged the office hours around the school schedule, and since the school is close by anyway, it has worked out well.

I treasure those priceless moments of companionship that I am able to spend with the girls. The mad dash from the playground to the car, the "girl talk" in the ice-cream parlor, and the window shopping arm-in-arm are happy times we will always remember.

As soon as we walk in the door at home, my training program goes into effect. At their young ages they have already seen how quickly outside activities thrust responsibilities upon them. Every grade brings an increased homework load. Piano lessons become more and more demanding. After-school athletics and plays take enormous blocks of time. An already-jammed schedule leaves little time for household tasks and personal quality time together. So I must have a plan to train them now for life so they will grow into independent and mature adults.

Set Boundaries With Latitude.   When children enter school, at times peer pressure and parental pressure clash. Regardless of what "the other kids" are doing, we know our values and intend to abide by them, and have confident expectation that our children will too.

Part of setting boundaries is saying *no.* I was amused at a cartoon which showed a small boy introducing himself to the little girl next door. "Hi," he said, "my name is 'No-No, Don't Touch,' what's yours?"

No can be such an ugly word to anyone, but especially to children. Since I must say it frequently, I try to avoid it whenever possible. Rather than saying *no* too often, I use phrases designed to soften the blow or redirect their actions, such as, "I'd rather you didn't," or "Let's do something else instead."

Work Before Play.   Charlie's grandmother, Mimi, who is eighty-four and one of my best friends, taught me a few lessons when I came into the Morgan family. Mimi could see that I obviously had little discipline for finishing my household chores each day. Time after time in a gentle but persuasive way, she would tell me, "If a job has to be done, it's best to do it immediately and get it out of the way."

I finally caught the idea, so now I'm passing it on, and my girls are catching it too. They have a routine each morning (it didn't come easily, if that's any comfort) and now the jobs they do are as natural as brushing their teeth. Since each girl has many jobs around the house, the rule is to finish their work before they play.

We give them responsibilities, as much and as fast as they can handle. These include cooking, cleaning their room, and taking care of their toys and belongings. When Michelle's favorite toy dog which walked and barked stopped dead in its tracks, she was quick to spot the problem. She told the store clerk her dog needed two batteries: "a walking battery and a talking battery!"

Make the Mundane Fun. Children have the marvelous capacity for seeing wonder in the commonplace. Make-believe and reality fit comfortably together in a child's mind. The parent who can join in make-believe recaptures the miracle of childhood, and gains the admiration and trust of his young.

When Michelle was three, Charlie tried to interest her in bringing in the newspaper each morning, without much success. Apparently, tramping across the wet grass or fishing in the shrubbery wasn't any more fun for her than it was for him!

One morning, he opened the front door and, with amazement in his voice, joked, "Michelle, you wouldn't believe who I just saw hopping away! I think it was the Paper Bunny! Do you want to run out and see what he brought?"

Michelle's eyes and mouth opened wide. She wasn't quite sure about it all. Suddenly she flew out the door, returning triumphantly with her prize.

She was hooked on the Paper Bunny for about a week, and though the intrigue wore off quickly and the morning paper became ordinary all too soon, I was proud of Charlie's ingenuity.

Edgar A. Guest once said, "I'd rather one should walk with me than merely show the way." Working alongside and being creative makes even the unpleasant bearable. Just as "a spoonful of sugar makes the medicine go down," so does a mother's happy attitude and a dad's Paper Bunny.

Even something as dreadful as the doctor's office, or as

traumatic as the hospital, can be made at least bearable by a little effort. When Michelle turned four, the doctor scheduled her for surgery and ordered hospitalization for a week. Mothers were also permitted to "room-in" at the hospital so, planning never to leave her side, I armed myself with books, puppets, and every sort of happy diversion. Michelle and I packed for our "vacation," and soon we were isolated in a sterile, most unhotel-like, green cubicle.

During those long days preceding and following the operation, I read and sang and danced and would have stood on my head, if I could, to keep Michelle's mind off her pain. Finally it was over. The wonderful check-out day arrived. As I carried the patient down the corridor, I asked her, "Well, honey, how did you like our vacation together?"

She looked at me very kindly and said, "It was nice, Mom." She hesitated, "But I think I like Disney World better!"

Correct the Overstep.   Discipline involves two parts. The first is setting reasonable boundaries for children, and the second, correcting them when the boundaries are overstepped. Step #2—correcting the overstep— certainly is not pleasant, but it is so necessary. For me the main reason is the scriptural admonition. We as parents are instructed to correct them, and our children are commanded to obey.

Novelist Taylor Caldwell believes that boys respect swift punishment and pain. They may yell and say some harsh things, but they will respect the lessons of "that good right hand which deals out immediate justice, as well as cookies and caresses." She warns that if discipline is not administered while the child is still young, the parents should expect trouble later on. "He will shriek *police brutality,*" writes Caldwell, "when he is given the blows he ought to have had in the playpen."

Authoress Betty Elliot tells of her rigorous disciplined life while growing up, where "a small switch was kept in nearly every room of the house, on the lintel of the door, and often my mother's eyes, raised in the direction of the door, galvanized us to obedience. But any one of the six children would be glad to testify to the rollicking fun we have always had, laughing most of the time."

At times it helps to give children a choice as to discipline. After repeated warnings, Lisa broke a glass tabletop. The thirteen-year-old was told, "You have been warned many times about your carelessness. Now do you want to pay twenty dollars for a new tabletop or do you want a spanking? Go to your room and think about it and when you decide, let me know."

When teens have a choice, they rarely think parents are unfair. P.S. She took the spanking.

Contrary to her dad's instructions, Carol drove the family car to her boyfriend's house after school. In private, her parents discussed her penalty, and agreed to take away her car privileges for one week.

Then they asked Carol what she thought they should do. She admitted her wrong and felt that two weeks would be fair. Since it was her first offense, Carol's parents kept the keys for ten days. Young people seem to always suggest a more severe discipline than parents do, proving over and over again that they do want limits.

In the Evening

Professor Keith J. Edwards of the Rosemead Graduate School of Psychology writes, "Nearly any American family is undergoing pressure from either (1) an overt family breakup (separation or divorce); (2) excessive mobility (the typical family in Southern California moves every three to five years); (3) self-centered recreational activity; or (4) the hardworking American male syndrome."

Togetherness.   When a frustrated mother took her moody twelve-year-old son to the doctor, she was surprised at his prescription. "This child doesn't need a shot," he said. "He needs an audience."

Being an audience is not always easy, but it's absolutely necessary in building confidence and happy memories and family "togetherness." It takes much time and patience and effort to be an audience in the midst of a whirlwind, last-minute, emergency-type of life that many Americans lead. Psychologist James Dobson wrote in *Hide or Seek,* ". . . There was a time when a man didn't fret if he missed a stage coach; he'd just catch it next month. Now if a fellow misses a section of a revolving door he's thrown into despair!

"But guess who is the inevitable loser from this breathless life-style?" he asks. "It's the little guy who is leaning against the wall with his hands in the pocket of his blue jeans." Dr. Dobson points out that when Mom promises to take the boy to the park, at the last minute her meetings always interfere. He tags around after his father saying, "Play ball, Dad!" But as usual, Dad's too pooped and besides, he always brings home a briefcase full of work. The message comes through loud and clear, says Dobson, "His folks are busy again. So he drifts into the family room and watches two hours of pointless cartoons and reruns on television."

Celebrate.   To make life exciting, Charlie and I prefer to create and celebrate with our children. A Total Woman celebrates with her family at least once a week, over anything and everything: for the cleanest room— a Happy Birthday—if Daddy gets home early—if Daddy gets home!

One of the special delights for me is teaching the girls to cook. In comparing modern food conveniences with the past, Sam Levenson writes, "Everything is prepared, presliced, precooked, preheated, prefabricated, premixed, prefrozen, prewhipped, premashed, prediced, preshrunk, presteamed, and pretested. The child's food is mashed, smashed, squashed, ground, filtered, homogenized, served on dishes shaped like windmills, turtles, bears, imprinted with nursery rhymes and puzzles, and must crackle, pop, whistle, talk, sing, and be eaten with itsy-bitsy portions up to graduation from high school."

Instead of all the convenience foods, I like to show the girls how to cook from scratch. Every afternoon is snack time. Laura and Michelle occasionally like to make yogurt Popsicles. My favorite is a yogurt sundae with strawberry jam and broken walnuts. This concoction gives me energy and a feeling of well-being, and holds me over to dinnertime. By the way, so many women have sent in super recipes that I plan to share these in a *Total Woman Cookbook,* some day soon.

Evenings consist of dinner and dishes and diversion. The dinner hours can be the highlight of the day. Children love the excitement of a picnic, the surprise of a candle in the potatoes, or a sparkler in the watermelon. Food coloring (the nonharmful variety) in the milk and cookies is also a great attention-grabber.

When having spaghetti or chow mein or tacos, I announce "night in Italy" (or whatever country) the day before. I am surprised by their improvised costumes, and the family also learns something about the country in the process.

One mother surprised her four-year-old by putting Bo-Bo, a favorite stuffed monkey in the high chair at dinner, complete with a place setting of china on the tray. Her little child was ecstatic.

Another family arranged "a night out" in their own dining room, transformed into "Davidson's Restaurant." Mom Davidson was the waitress and Daddy the chef. The children ordered from a prepared menu, including the "Specialty of the House" at a bargain price. Now the two preschoolers want to "eat out" lots.

The Reynolds, neighbors of the Davidsons, dubiously tried "eating-out-in" with their tough baseball stars, ages nine and twelve. Their reply, "Great, Mom, let's do this once a week!" Mom almost fainted!

After dinner and dishes is family-fun time. Charlie and I make a special effort to spend time with our children. At their young age, they don't seem to care what we do as long as we do it together—even if it's grocery shopping.

Create.   In an editorial for *Newsweek* magazine, Robert Mayer facetiously suggested a different kind of family hour: ". . . I propose that for 60 to 90 minutes each evening, right after the early-evening news, *all television broadcasting in the United States be prohibited by law.*"

Television fixation has become addictive and hypnotic to millions of children of all ages. The side effects are twofold: First of all, creativity is stifled. I don't know of any great work of art or music or literature which was created during a soap opera. According to Mayer, there is more entertainment and intellectual nourishment in a decent book than in a month of typical TV programming. In an attempt to find nourishment in the same level of comedy, drama, or entertainment, for Suzie, Johnny, Pop, and Grandma, the result is the lowest common denominator, that being a twelve-year-old-chewing-gum mentality.

Second, the input received is often negative, "a red-meat diet of slaughter, mayhem, and murder." Mayer also notes that psychological studies indicate that children exposed to this diet night after night tend to become disturbed and more prone to violence themselves.

A world of positive alternatives is available to help create creative children. Good books can become your child's good friends, if only they are introduced to each other. If you love to read, you have already discovered that reading is one of life's great pleasures. Complete libraries are located within reach of most any American. Paperback books now make classics and expensive hardback books available at a fraction of their original cost. A veritable gold mine of information is at the fingertips of any child or his parents.

Good books stimulate creativity. Our girls have library cards and each of them takes out eight books at a time. The more they begin to read, the more they begin to write. It seems to be directly related. Now they have both begun writing their own books with separate chapters on "My Friends," "My Family," and "My School." The pages go into a notebook we keep for them, and they are so proud of it.

Word games and crossword puzzles help expand their vocabulary. Logic and numbers games stimulate their analytical processes. Crafts help develop hand coordination. The girls make their own birthday cards, shadowboxes, puppet shows, and scrapbooks. They keep a small supply of construction paper, tape, string, Magic Markers, and the like, and their imagination never ceases to amaze me.

We set aside playtime with lots of laughter and roughhousing, so in a quiet moment they will be willing to listen to our point of view on life, love, and happiness.

Children not only love to play, they also love to act. Our girls are really stagestruck, and make up little plays once they are encouraged and shown how.

Talent shows are a real family highlight. Talents range from gymnastic displays to piano concerts. When "Talent Night" is announced they scramble around and prepare for hours, usually on a project together. Occasionally, on "Homemade TV Night" Michelle is the weather girl, who tells us whether it rained that day. Laura plays Barbara Walters, and puts Michelle through the third degree.

Magic shows are often the funniest of all. Several years ago Laura and Charlie did a rope trick together, and I asked how they did it. Charlie told Laura that a good magician never tells her secrets, to which Laura replied, "Oh, come on, let's tell her, Dad. After all, she *is* our mother."

Music also plays a big part in our girls' lives. They both play the piano and have even composed little songs of their own. They perform when company comes and slowly are acquiring poise and confidence before other audiences.

And at Bedtime

Just before putting our children to bed, we set aside time for spiritual nourishment. If we're going out for the evening, it's not always feasible, but whenever possible we all have this time together. Charlie and I believe a spiritual foundation will give our girls the confidence that nothing else on earth can give. Knowing that God loves them, and has a wonderful plan for them gives them stability in the face of temptation.

We play games, read the Bible, and pray. The games are usually Bible-related, such as "Twenty Questions," when we all try to guess a Bible object or person in the allotted time. Michelle once stumped us all with "the smallest thing in the Bible"—a germ. I had to disqualify myself from the game when she whispered to me, "Mom, does a germ go to the bathroom?"

Last week Charlie asked the girls to name a Bible person for each letter of the alphabet. Michelle bogged down on some letters and finally filled in *Ahab* and *Ohab* and *Zohab* and *Cathlick*.

The Bible, My Friend.   The time spent reading the Bible each night ranks as top priority because we know the importance of planting the Divine Word early. We read from The Living Bible—a chapter from the Old Testament at night, and a chapter from the New Testament at breakfast. We read straight through to see the pattern developing.

Reading the Bible each day may sound deadly, but our goal is to make it practical, not ritual. We vary the place where we read, sometimes lying on our bed, or in the living room, or occasionally under the stars with a flashlight.

Before reading, Charlie reviews by asking questions about the night before. Michelle sometimes has her own paraphrase—like David's killing Goliath with his pet rock!

Both she and Laura interrupt all the time to ask questions such as, "Why did God do that?" If they don't ask questions, Charlie does. We are not as concerned about the distance from the Dead Sea to Mount Sinai, as we are the lessons being taught, and how they apply in school, in the kitchen, and in the office today. As we read about the children of Israel wandering through the wilderness into the Promised Land, we can apply the lessons they learned to our own lives.

Talking to God.   After the Scripture is read, we pray for all our problems and our friends and for "good dreams." Nothing makes prayer time as exciting as an *answer* to prayer.

Michelle's first answered prayer was a thrill to us all. When she was very little, she and I spent one afternoon lying in our hammock watching fluffy clouds glide by. She said, "I wish the sky would turn pink."

I said, "Maybe the Lord would paint a pink sunset for you tonight. Do you want to ask Him?"

Fascinated with the thought of asking and receiving, she prayed fervently, "Dear Jesus, will You make a pink sunset for me tonight?" I prayed silently and earnestly, too. "Lord, she's only a little child and this will make such an impression if You do this. *Please* do it."

All afternoon she was so excited, and so was I. I'm not advising other people to ask such glib requests of God, but for us that day it was the right thing to do.

With the hustle of putting dinner on the table, Michelle and I sat down with the family, forgetting com-

pletely about her prayer. We had nearly finished dinner
when Laura glanced out the window and said, "Wow!
Look at the sunset!" We all looked up at the rosiest,
glowingest sunset I had ever seen—many shades of pink
vibrantly colored the western sky.

Michelle was absolutely awestruck. Excitedly, she told
of her prayer that afternoon, and we all reveled in God's
answer to a little girl. I knew Michelle would never forget that sunset—her first answered prayer—and the fact
that she knew her God cared personally about *her*.

At night we alternate who prays. Sometimes we all do,
sometimes just one or two. Our prayers aren't formal; we
just talk to God. Then we hug and snuggle, and they fall
into bed with a smile.

11   Joy Forever

Sir William Gladstone once asked his young nephew, "What do you plan to do with your life, John?"

"I want to study law, Uncle William," he replied.

"And then what?" asked Sir William.

"Well, then I hope to be an apprentice and observe my colleagues well, and become a reputable lawyer."

"Then what?" queried Gladstone.

"Well, I suppose I shall look for a wife and raise a family."

"Then what?" persisted Gladstone.

Somewhat exasperated, young John sputtered a bit, and said, "Well, I'll acquire a fortune and make a good life, and. . . ."

"And then what?" came the same question.

Completely unnerved, he blustered, "Well, I guess I'll *die*!"

Sir William Gladstone gently asked, "And then what?"

For many years, I asked myself that question, "And then what?" I was concerned about eternity, and disturbed at how fleeting this life seemed in comparison. Maybe I'd be here for twenty more years. Or forty, or sixty, but then what? At times, my head hurt and my heart hurt. I felt empty inside. The Bible expressed my feelings succinctly, "Though a man lives a thousand years twice over, but doesn't find contentment—well, what's the use?"[21]

I didn't know my reason for being, or the purpose of this life, or the purpose afterward. Not that I didn't try to find the good life. I had romance and honors and pleasure, but they never satisfied.

The Search Goes On

A search means you haven't found what you're looking for. For me that was meaning and love and joy. Other women have admitted that they are longing for the same intangibles; I understand. I remember the darkness.

"I'm coping with changes in my relationship with my husband," wrote one. "Physically and emotionally, I'm a wreck. My teenagers put me down and my little one tries my patience. I'm trying to graciously accept this stage of life and go from here. I believe in God, but I don't grasp what life is all about. The hardest part of all, I don't understand *why* I am here."

For *Martha* the search is insistent. "You started in me a burning desire to know why I'm here. I am a church-goer, not devout but searching. A voice keeps pounding in my head. There's a purpose for my being that I have not yet discovered."

For *Linda* the search is lonely. "I am so very mixed up," she wrote. "I have lost my way, and I'm reaching out my hand to you. My family and everyone else have given up on me. That's why I took the overdose."

For *Beverly* the search aches. She has a lovely home in Oklahoma and a ski house in Colorado. She's a member of the Junior League, Kappa Alpha Theta, and all the other social things you can name. "But most of all," she wrote, "I have a big empty space inside that needs to be filled up. I'm grasping for the Power Source."

For *Gail* the search is internal. "I know your ideas work, but I also know me. I speak before I think. I get angry easily. In short, I don't have the inner peace you talk about. I knew before I read your book that what was wrong with my life was inside myself."

For *Bonnie* the search seems hopeless. "I was and am a forlorn person. I will never be a happy person. I feel I am doomed to hell here on earth, and hell is all I have to look forward to after I die."

And the search goes on, haunting the midstream American woman, and the prominent woman, and the quiet-in-the-shadows woman.

One Long Road

Kay and I had been at the beach together. Returning to the car we stopped at an open-air fruit stand for a drink. The proprietor seemed grateful for two customers, not because we paid but because we listened. He seemed so sad. As we talked about life, he summed up his philosophy in one line, "I go to work to earn the dough to buy the bread to get the strength to go to work again."

More customers came, and we left our new friend squeezing oranges. Driving home Kay stared straight ahead, not saying a word. Finally I asked, "What's the matter?"

"Oh, I don't know," she mused. "I was thinking about that man and what he said. That's my life too. Exactly. Something's wrong inside me. I have all these *things* but I'm not really living. I guess I'm looking for the ultimate."

I didn't know Kay too well, since we had recently met at a class, but I was surprised at her remark. She was beautiful and obviously very wealthy. I had heard her talk of week-long retreats to famous spas to keep her absolutely flawless figure.

"Kay," I asked, "how in the world could you identify with the orange-juice man with everything you have? You've probably never worked a day in your life."

She thought for a moment, then said, "Oh, it's not his work—it's the hopeless going in circles." Her life was full and fantastic—the best that money could buy—but it wasn't enough. Her body was satiated but her spirit was starving, and she felt it. She felt the pain keenly. She knew there was something more.

"Kay," I told her, "the only one who can give you real meaning to life is God. And anyone who searches for God with all his heart will find Him."[22]

"I believe in God," she interrupted. "I keep the Ten Commandments. I'm religious."

"I'm not talking about religion. That's what man does to try to please God. It doesn't work. God isn't interested in our religion—He's interested in a relationship with us. He knows us and wants us to know Him. God loves *you*, Kay, and has a super plan for your life."

"But He seems so nebulous," she said, "so distant. Sometimes I feel so terribly alone, even with groups of people."

"I understand your loneliness," I told her, "so does He. You are lonely because you are separated from God—separated because of sin."

She admitted she felt separated but didn't like to think she sinned. I agreed, "I don't like it either, Kay, but we all fall short of God's perfection. You may lead the best life in the world, but that's not good enough."

Kay swallowed, and I knew the point had hit home. I, too, never realized I needed a Saviour—until I saw I was lost. At that point I was utterly without hope. Life seemed but one long road between two hospitals.

"My search ended with a Saviour," I told her. "The true Passover Lamb. His name is Jesus. He paid the penalty for what you and I have done wrong. He paid with His blood. God's gift of eternal life wasn't tied in yellow ribbons, but with spikes driven into a wooden cross. You may know that, but do you know Him? He alone can put joy in your heart."

We arrived at Kay's house, and as she got out of the car, she put her arm around me and looked at me with eyes full of tears.

It was time to go. "Kay, dear, if you believe what He said, He'll give you what He promised. Your Creator will become your Saviour."

It broke my heart to drive away. I knew she was in labor—spiritual labor—and I hurt for her. I thought about her until the phone rang the next morning.

It was Kay and she was joyous. "I did it, Marabel! I talked to God this morning and said, 'Sir, I'm not real sure about what I've been learning. I'm not even sure of Your name. Marabel says it's *Jesus,* and if that's so, that's what I'll call You, but will You please show me for sure.' Then I asked Jesus into my life as my Messiah, my Saviour! I feel such peace. Thank you, thank you for telling me how."

That was five years ago. I wish you could see Kay today. Since that time she has experienced overwhelming heartache, including a divorce. When her husband married Kay's best friend, Kay remained stable and serene. Her friends single her out and ask her, "What's happened to you? Any other person would be a basket case if they'd gone through what you have, yet you're radiant. How can you do it?"

And she tells them she doesn't know what tomorrow holds, but she knows who holds tomorrow.

Something Is Missing

Several weeks ago, a confused military wife wrote telling of her inner turmoil. "I'm all mixed up inside," she said. "I want to know the joy and peace you speak of. I want to give my love freely to my husband and children. I'm desperate. I feel as if something is missing no matter what I do."

The ache of that woman's heart is universal. The ache comes from being on the outside looking in—like a child looking in the candy-store window. Something is missing, but what?

Getting married or raising children doesn't completely fulfill a woman. Having a career does not produce peace. Neither prestige nor power brings purpose. Money can't make a happy atmosphere at the breakfast table. Education can't take away the lump in your throat or the ache in your heart. Nothing that man can do can prevent sickness, or disappointment, or death.

What is the purpose of it all? I believe a woman is just spinning her wheels until she is fulfilled by the Ultimate, God Himself. He is the only One who can get it all together. He is the only One who can keep it there. He is the only One who can make you complete—*total.* He is the only One who can give you a good attitude all the time. And best of all, He offers to you the possibility of a life of no regrets.

His name: Jesus of Nazareth, the God-Man.

In the words of Frank William Boreham in *Drums of Dawn,* "Sir Christopher Wren expressed himself in granite; Joseph Turner expressed himself in oils; Michelangelo expressed himself in marble; Shakespeare expressed himself in ink; but God selected *flesh* as the ideal vehicle for self-expression. And there is nothing so eloquent as flesh." The Word was made flesh. God became man.

Jesus is the only person who won't betray your trust. He understands your situation implicitly. He is trustworthy, sufficiently powerful, and *shockproof.* And besides, He already knows.

A beautiful spiritual transaction occurs when a mortal woman tells an immortal Saviour what's bothering her. The burden passes somehow from her shoulders to His. He whispers in her mind, "Dare to trust Me." And timidly she assents *yes,* and peace comes. Her circumstances may still be the same, but she isn't. He doesn't promise a cure; He does promise a new perspective.

People who practice a positive thinking, self-hypnotic, conjured-up pep talk may claim to have the same peace, but there is such a difference. One is *self-imposed* and thereby, dreadfully limited; the other is *God-imposed* and superabundantly unlimited.

Why do people think life on earth will go on forever? The fact of certain death lies ahead, but how to face it? Ironically, a woman isn't prepared to live until she's prepared to die. Only Jesus of Nazareth can take care of the fear of dying *and* the fear of living. He's the only One who conquered both. He's been there.

As songwriter-pianist Tedd Smith wrote in *Decision* magazine, "Because He died, I can live. Oh, sure, I'll

meet the phonies, the 'grab-all-you-can-and-shove-it-in-
the-bank' Jonies. But that's not my scene. I know what
it can mean to find new life, new hope, new purpose—
and stop my runnin'!"

Icing on the Cake

Catherine went to the doctor two weeks before Christmas complaining of black moods and fainting spells.
"Nothing wrong," the doctor said, "except you're too
tired." He sent her home for total rest until Christmas.
After she wept all week, the doctor said, "You're simply
depressed, Catherine."

"I have a good husband, a beautiful three-year-old
daughter, and no debts to pay," she told herself. "Why
am I depressed?"

She saw a psychologist. He suggested that she was
"setting her goals too high and expecting too much of
others."

Back to the doctor she went, this time for antidepres-
sants. "They didn't make a lot of difference, except they
enabled me to tuck all my little problems into packages
to be opened later, one at a time, until all of them were
cleaned up."

And then she described her change. "Your Scripture
references helped me realize how much I really need
God, even when I'm feeling resentful. When I grabbed
hold of the Lord's hand, I went off the pills I was taking
and I feel fabulous! My marriage has been rejuvenated.
My husband told me it was as if we were just married

again. My life has changed so much—since I plugged into the Power Source."

So many letters have poured in telling the same story. Lani was rescued from the depths. *"Thank you,* like I've never said it before. Your book came to me just as my life was in total despair. The only thing that held me, my husband, and four children together was revenge. We were in a contest to see who could hurt each other the most. How miserable we all were!

"Finally I hit rock bottom. I screamed out to God and He helped me. I opened the door! I surrendered my whole self to God and my whole life was changed! I have a reason to go on. Now the Light shines bright and warm in my heart. Jesus is the 'icing on the cake' of my life."

The Son shines in, dispelling the darkness. Barbara wrote, "At last I have found that happiness and inner peace. For some reason I'm reminded of a song by Roger Miller that goes:

'Look'ee, Look'ee, I can see a ray of sunshine
    shining;
I can feel a rainbow coming deep inside my mind;
I can feel my cares and troubles falling all around
    me;
I'm glad the sunshine found me. I know I've been
    hard to find.' "

Lynn wrote that for many, many years she had been crying out to God, begging, pleading with Him, sometimes ignoring Him. "Little did I ever know that while reading your story of how you searched that I would at last unbolt the door to my heart and accept my Saviour!

"Just before this happened, something I read clicked in my heart. I looked up and whispered, 'I'm getting closer.' I read on, and before I knew it, I was standing straight up out of my chair! My heart was filled with so much love and joy I thought I would burst. I'm *alive*, Marabel Morgan. There is just so much more that I want to tell you, that I could go on forever! And I will!"

Fickle Fate

Maria, a secretary from New Mexico, had been going with Jose for seven months. "He acts like it's all over," she wrote, "but he still comes to see me and even makes love to me. I'm very poor and don't have a good body and I know I'm not attractive to him."

Scared to death of losing Jose, Maria wrote for advice. "I'd be unhappy for the rest of my life and I might even commit suicide, because what would I live for? I'd lose my own life because he is my life. Please help me before it's too late. He is the only key to my happiness."

When a boyfriend or a husband is "the only key to happiness," it's dangerous to get out of bed in the morning. An Ohio State University researcher estimated that 85 percent of all American marriages are terminated either in the courts or in the heart. Sooner or later husbands and boyfriends may bring disillusionment. And then what?

Life too is fickle. Emotions are so unstable, they

change from phone call to phone call. Heartache can come at every turn in the road.

Nancy, a working wife with three young boys, can testify to that. Three years ago her mother died of cancer. Two years ago her twenty-five-year-old husband died of the same disease. In the midst of her grief, Nancy remarried last year only to find that her present husband has Bell's palsy. As if that isn't enough, Nancy's father is now in the hospital with cancer. In utter despair, Nancy wrote, "I don't know if I can take any more of this. I just came from the doctor and found that I have cervical cancer, which will require an operation next week. I feel that my marriage must work," she added. "Please help me. I need some sort of encouragement and outside help."

Like Nancy, I too need encouragement and outside help. When problems come, I know that there's no way I am able to cope in my own strength. I try to do it sometimes, but I'm powerless and weak.

The key to handling my problems is to discern between happiness and joy. For me it's a constant struggle to recognize the differences between these two terms—which are so often used interchangeably—but have meanings which are poles apart.

Happiness is . . . a crackling fireplace, a licking puppy, a tender teenage kiss. Happiness is a child's laughter on Christmas morning. Happiness is good news from home, red roses, a lover's touch. Happiness is Aunt Bertha canceling her two-week visit.

Happiness is fickle. Happiness (or the lack of it) is contingent on the moment, the boyfriend, the husband, the doctor's report. Happiness is unpredictable. Happiness is illusive. *If only I could get married. . . . If only I could get single. . . . If only. . . .* Happiness depends on people and circumstances, but people and circumstances often change unexpectedly. *Poof,* and the best laid plans go up in smoke.

Fullness of Joy

Joy. That's where Jesus comes in. Joy, in contrast to happiness, does not depend on husbands or health or circumstances, but rather on a relationship with God. My joy depends solely upon Him who said, "These things have I spoken unto you, that *my* joy might remain in you, and that *your* joy might be full."[23] The joy of God Almighty, constant and reliable and all encompassing, becomes my own joy. Not bits and pieces—but full. Complete. Total.

He promises to supply *all* my needs. When I go to Him admitting my lack, He fills me up. He alone restores my soul. Secure in His love, I know who I really am, a child of the King. At last, free. Truly liberated. As Jesus said, "If the Son therefore shall make you free, ye shall be free indeed."[24]

When I invited Jesus of Nazareth into my life, I became a child in His Forever Family, forgiven and assured of life eternal.

And that wasn't all. God also had a plan for my life and what a plan! I started down the road on a great adventure, which He calls "the abundant life."[25] Jesus Himself said, "If you abide in me and my words abide in you, you shall ask what you will, and it shall be done unto you. . . . Ask and you shall receive that your joy may be full."[26]

I have learned the condition to having constant joy. The condition is allowing Jesus to sit at the control center of my life. To relinquish those controls, I say, "Jesus my Lord, please guide me in Your perfect plan today."

As I pick up the Bible each morning, I ask Him to teach me as I read. I don't want to depend on my feelings, or whether I slept well, or stayed up with the baby half the night. If I depend on His sure Word of truth, no matter what comes, I'll know I'm in His plan. God isn't asking for a tip-top performance from me—just a willingness on my part. That takes the pressure off.

At times I take the controls back, but I'm always sorry I did. I have "tasted" the abundant life—the life of joy that Jesus lives through me—and that's the life I want. As King David expressed it, "Show me the path of Life; in your presence is fullness of joy."[27]

Valley of the Shadow

A few years after we were married, I became pregnant for the second time. I was thrilled and began to dream of the idyllic days when we would be "four."

Abruptly my dream shattered when the baby arrived a month early. "She is a fighter, fighting for her life," my doctor said, "but the chances are very slim." Stunned, I couldn't really comprehend what he was saying. How could this be? My baby certainly was going to live—she couldn't die! Besides, I was a believer and really loved God with all my heart. He would never let such a thing happen to me.

I prayed for my baby earnestly but never really felt fearful. I smugly felt that God and I were on such good terms that there was just no need to worry. Everyone else was worried, including the doctor, but I reassured them all that she would be just fine.

Finally my little girl, at last exhausted, gave up the fight. My husband heard the news first. White-faced and trembling, he told me she had died. When he tried to comfort me, I turned away from him to sob out my grief alone. I simply could not accept it.

My baby was dead. How could this happen to me? Why? Why? Bitterness welled up toward God. I felt as if He had slapped me hard across the face. But immediately I "heard" that familiar quiet voice down in my soul, "Marabel, don't you know that I love you?" And my soul responded, "Yes, Lord," and I did know it.

Even though my plans were scrapped and my world had fallen in, God was there and still in control, and I whispered through my tears, "Jesus, I know You love me. I will trust You." I felt the loss just as keenly as before, and yet now I knew God had control of the situation. Though I continued to cry, I felt peace.

Then an odd thing occurred. I was aware that deep down inside my innermost being, joy was pushing up through me. The only way I know to describe it is a bubble of joy. I was shocked. How could I feel joy when my baby had just died? It was barbaric, and yet the joy kept coming until I thought I would burst out laughing —for joy.

Suddenly I realized. Jesus was showing me once again that He alone is my Source of joy. He can take an awful situation, a hopeless situation such as death, and bring joy in the midst.

God was able to turn sorrow into joy. Heaven became much more real, because I had someone there waiting for me. My little girl is there and we're all anxious to be there with her. The certainty of that family reunion when we step over into eternity takes the sting out of death. When I check out here, life has just begun.

Any Woman Can

Last year, while driving home from vacation in the mountains, we covered four states in one day. That night as we put the weary little travelers to bed, Charlie said, "Michelle, today we had breakfast in North Carolina, lunch in South Carolina, dinner in Georgia, and we're sleeping in Florida tonight. Which state did you like the best?"

Michelle reached up from her bed to hug her daddy. She smiled happily, obviously enjoying the moment and piped, "Daddy, I like whatever state I'm in right now the best!"

Saint Paul said it this way almost two thousand years earlier, ". . . I have learned in whatsoever state I am, therewith to be content."[28]

And that's the secret of life: living contentedly in the moment—not dwelling on the good ol' days, nor wistfully dreaming about what might be, but living now, *today.*

Any woman who is filled with joy, His joy, can also tell her Heavenly Father, "I like whatever state I'm in right now the best." And not just *tell* Him—but shout for joy!

Assignment

1. *Peace Talks*—Listen and Learn
Starting tomorrow morning, try these suggestions on your husband or your closest friend for one day:

    A.   Only give constructive and positive comments in spite of what you hear him say. Bite your tongue if you start to snap back. Remember that if you answer his angry words with your angry words, it is the second words that make the quarrel.

    B.   Ask him to explain in simple language one aspect of his job you never fully understood. Let him know you think he is important. Then watch the atmosphere change.

2. *All in the Family*—Listen and Love
Make bedtime for the children a "love-in." Try to be

totally available for them at least twenty minutes twice a week. Talk with them about their day and their plans for tomorrow. Discuss their "time" needs and help them organize.

3. *Joy Forever*—Listen and Live

A.   For instructions on a *new life,* read and apply chapter 5 of First John, verses 9–13 in the Bible.

B.   For instructions on a *new joy,* read and apply chapters 15 and 16 of Saint John.

12 Conclusion

While teaching a seminar in an eastern city, I assigned some "homework" for the ladies to apply at home that night. Most of the women hurried out the doors of the auditorium eager to start, but one beautiful young woman approached me, literally shaking with fury. "I can't do these assignments," she glowered. "My husband and I are hardly speaking to each other."

I replied, "Okay! Okay! You don't have to. You don't have to do any of the things we talked about."

She relaxed a bit but was still trembling. "I'll tell you what. I'll give you an easy assignment," I grinned. "I know you can take a bath." I paused and she said, "Hummph! Well, of course!"

"All right," I said, "Just take a bath and put on something comfortable tonight."

She looked slightly relieved, so I decided to take the plunge. "One other thing, if you want to. You can cook, can't you?" Again that miffed snort, "Well, of course!"

"All right, cook a simple dinner. Make it easy on yourself; anything will do. That's your assignment. Take a bath, and prepare an easy dinner."

She looked apprehensive. I wanted to put my arms around her and say, "Hey, everything's going to be all right, believe me." But I couldn't. It wouldn't have done any good. She had to see for herself.

Laurie went home that day and thought it over. The principles of love cannot be taught, they have to be "caught," and somewhere along the line she "caught" them. She took a bath, put on new party pajamas for her husband, then cooked a roast, and made dinner extra-special with tablecloth, candles—the works!

At six o'clock, she and the dinner were ready, but no husband appeared. Six-thirty came and went. No husband. Seven o'clock, not a word. Eight o'clock, but nary a phone call to say where he was.

For three hours, Laurie vacillated back and forth between fury and poise. Paul had been late so many times before, but somehow she thought this night would be different. She began to wonder if she shouldn't call it quits once and for all.

Finally, a little after nine o'clock he sauntered in, completely unconcerned. At that moment, she had determined to keep calm even though it took everything she had. Her husband gave no explanation for being late as they sat down to the dinner, which Laurie had kept warm. She served his plate instead of her usual harangue, and asked about his day.

After a few minutes, Paul looked at her and said, "Hey, what's the matter with you? Why aren't you crabbing the way you usually do?"

Quietly, Laurie replied earnestly, "I love you and I want to be a good wife to you. And, I'm trying!"

Paul looked stunned. He sat still for a moment. Then he got up from the table and came around to Laurie. He knelt down beside her, put his head on her lap, and began to sob. "Last night," she reported to the class that next morning, "was the best night we've ever had in our marriage!"

About eight months later I met Laurie again. She was vibrant but realistic. "It's been awfully hard going," she said after we'd talked a while, "but we're going to make it!"

Henpecked Henry

Most of the women I've talked with also want to make it. They want a happy marriage. The only variable is *how.*

One question I'm frequently asked by women who are considering a change from nag to lover is, "What if I do all these things for my husband, but he never responds, and I get left holding the bag?"

That's a fair question—and an honest one—and I suggest that it be answered with a question. If your marriage isn't everything you ever hoped it would be, and if you want it to be just super, what are your alternatives right now?

Here come the options again. They are usually two-fold: to nag or to love. You may recall from the *Introduction* that the principles of this book assume that if you're married, you want your marriage to succeed. These suggestions are intended to help a marriage and make it sizzle and thus, the option of splitting up is not included.

We are left then with two alternatives: to nag or to love. If "to nag" is your bag, the next question is whether your way is working.

If Henpecked Henry is happy at home, then keep it up. But if he's not, then what? If all else has failed, how about love as a last resort? Love is an alternative, regardless of whether you have tried it, and if you *haven't,* you will never know what love might have done.

"If the whole world turns against me," says the Reverend Steve Brown, "love is knowing that one person cares . . . one person I can depend on . . . one person who is not in competition with me . . . one person who always wills the best . . . where I can go when I am wounded and know I'll be healed . . . where I don't have to wear a mask or be dishonest . . . where I can say anything and know that I'll be accepted. Now that's love, and that's when two people become one."

"But my marriage is too far gone," a woman from Denver wrote. "I'd like for us to stay together, but there's just no hope. Besides you don't know my husband. He's something else!"

Many women have written telling about their seem-

ingly impossible situation at home. In one letter contain-
ing eighteen pages of how horrid hubby was, the writer
asked, "Now, don't you agree I should leave him?"

I can't answer her question with a *yes* or *no* for several
reasons. First of all, being married to a lawyer, I know
there are at least two sides to every story—my way and
"the wrong way"—and often a third way: the truth! No
matter how terrible the case sounds, Awful Andy is entitled to be heard before being condemned. And after all,
his wife must have had some good reason to marry him,
so he can't be all bad.

Second, I'm not playing God. Only He knows what's
possible. Besides, sometimes even the wife herself deep
down doesn't want a divorce. At the close of that lady's
letter was a P.S. which read, "I love him and would die
if he ever left me."

Far be it for me to encourage a quickie burial when
the patient is not yet dead.

Phoebe Revisited

On the road to Mend-a-Marriage, you can also count
on Phoebe Phobia to strike fear at the most unexpected
time. Whenever she sees joy, that old defeater loves to
intimidate and snatch it away. She asks such questions as:
"Love that creep? Are you kidding? Why should you
give in to him first? What about *your* rights?"

Her searching questions touch the very heart of your
actions. *Why* are you doing it anyway? For what you will
get, or for the joy of *giving?*

If you are only giving to get, Phoebe will wipe you out. But if your motive is love out of a pure heart, then the One who gives continued joy can answer those questions and chase Ms. Phobia away. The choice of which one you listen to is yours alone.

Phoebe will try to discourage you at every turn. Learn to recognize her subtle tactics designed to clog your heart with jealousy and bitterness and rob you of your joy. You will not be surprised when so-called friends attack, or your husband doesn't respond. You won't succumb to defeat.

A wife in the Mountain States had just discovered her husband's affair of two years. Although she felt completely deserted and unloved, she did admit that the affair was as much her fault as his.

She and her husband had tried wife-swapping with some friends. Then in the confusion afterwards, no one could unravel his feelings or emotions. After some months of soul-searching, she read *The Total Woman* at work, and went home "feeling so excited, happy, cheerful and determined to make our marriage the happiest one on earth."

That night when her husband came home, she helped him with the yard work until dark. She complimented him on his research project at the office, and they stayed up talking until after midnight.

That next night was her regular weekly visit to the marriage counselor who, upon hearing her enthusiasm, told her she was "just a slave." She wrote to ask, "How can a woman become a slave by showing her unconditional love for her husband?" I don't know how, if she chooses to do it.

The counselor recommended that she should come in for group therapy without her husband "to try to get over her fear of 'relating' to people." She wrote, "I don't feel like a freak just because I enjoy having my husband at home and worry when he's out drinking. Just because I don't approve of his going out and running the roads, and don't like to tell a bunch of strangers my problems, does this mean I don't relate?"

Phoebe Phobia comes in many forms. Of course, not all marriage counselors are Phoebe incognito, but her devious disguises make her so subtle—even in a counselor at times.

In his office *Mr.* Phobia literally destroyed this vulnerable homemaker. She said, "I want our marriage to work, but I'm becoming a nervous witch. We were both miserable tonight, and I have lost the desire to cheer him up—when only a few hours earlier I would have bent over backwards to make him happy."

Letting Go

Which brings us back to the beginning. Sometimes I don't have the desire either. It's so easy at times to allow another person to control my attitude and deflate me. The question then is who wins out, Phoebe Phobia or God Himself? If fear or intimidation is the force, it's not God, for the Scriptures say, "For God hath not given us a spirit of fear; but of power, and of love, and of a sound mind."[29] With *Him* I can go on, "even though." With an attitude like that, most husbands can't refuse. And even if mine should, then what? I have done all I could have done, and that's all anyone can do.

A single girl from Pennsylvania found that all her pet theories of love and marriage had been turned upside down. "I realize I've got a lot of changing to do—at least where attitudes and pure selfish love are concerned—but I want to change, even though it may mean no pot of gold at the end of the rainbow. I want to please Tom, but more than that, I want to be true to myself."

Another lady wrote shortly after her husband died of cancer. She said caring for him with love and tenderness was only possible because of the recent change in her life. After twenty-six years, ". . . the last few since I took your class were the happiest, even during the time of his illness. Before he died he kept whispering, 'Honey, I love you so much.' Having no regrets made it so much easier to let him go."

The Stalemate

The question in so many marriages is simply who (if any) is willing to make the first move towards restoring love. If you are caught in a vicious circle, you can step out of the circle anytime you choose. Phyllis wrote to say, "Thank you, thank you, thank you. Today after eight years of marriage, I received my first hello kiss. I would have melted right on the spot, but I decided I wanted to be around for more and more."

She and Mike had been in a stalemate for eight years. "That was me," she said, "the Stale Mate. Neither of us was willing to initiate love. Year after year I kept waiting for all the romance to come. All the time my darling Mike was waiting, too. Had I waited for him to change, it might have been another ten years. Love is like a wagon wheel. Someone has to *start* it going."

Other darling Mikes are also waiting. In Texas one "Mike" said, "Reading the bad examples in your book seemed almost like a road map of our marriage, and my heart just cried for the could-have-beens. My 'ex' stated that she married me to change me. And she could have, very easily, by just applying the four *A*s."

Still another Mike wrote, this one from the state prison in Pennsylvania. "I found drugs an easy way out, because I didn't know how to deal with our situation. The whole time we have been married, we never sat down and had a husband-and-wife talk. Not because I didn't want to, but because every time I tried she always had something smart to say. She speaks without thinking. I love her but she hurt me in so many ways. I am thirty-three, she is twenty-seven."

In an age where it often seems easier to split up than make up, it takes courage to try again. "The whole country," according to Nan Birmingham in *Town and Country* magazine, "seems to be involved in an old-fashioned college-freshman mixer, with masses of people mingling." The by-products of all this mingling are more than seven million stepchildren in the United States today.

The most bizarre trade in baseball history occurred several years ago when New York Yankee players Fritz Peterson and Mike Kekich traded their wives and four children and two dogs and two homes. "This wasn't a wife swap," both men emphasized, "it was a life swap."

Months later, Mike Kekich was alone, without wife or children. "I am the loser," he told the media. "To me there is nothing more important than a well-balanced family that lives, plays, and grows together. There is so much to be learned from each other. I miss my children.

"I have learned from the experience, believe me," he continued to reflect. "I have a couple of friends having marital problems. I have told them to hang on to any thread of happiness they have left on which to build."

Your marriage may be at the crossroads of Love and Splitsville, but whether it is hanging on by a thread or a rope, I believe where there's life, there's hope.

Any Thread Will Do

One Tuesday night, Don came home late from the plant. Since he was a supervisor, it was not unusual for him to work overtime. He wasn't hungry and appeared restless, as he picked at his dinner.

Finally, pushing his plate aside, he told Gail his problem. He had been having an affair with a girl at work, not just once, but for the past three years. Don said he had filed for divorce that day, and planned to remarry as soon as possible. The honeymoon was planned, the apartment leased, the furniture bought.

Gail was stunned to think he had already planned a whole new life with another woman, right under her nose. Looking back on her eight-year marriage, Gail said she had always patted herself on the back for putting up with his unusually heavy schedule and late hours. Meanwhile, Don thought she was so capable that he simply wasn't necessary anymore. He had found a woman who made him feel wanted and needed and like a man.

Even though she felt her marriage was finished, she resolved to change her own attitude instead of condemning him. Within a short time, she began to see results.

Her husband was stunned at her complete reversal. He began spending more and more time at home. One night he said, "At last I believe in miracles. I've seen one happen in front of my own eyes. You are transformed."

"He has come home for good," she wrote, "unbelievable as it may seem. I still have a lot to learn about being a friend, lover, and companion, but you and I and God have won! I can make it now that I found the keys—hope and courage."

Those two life-changing ingredients—hope and courage. Hope involves faith and courage involves attitude. Hope is His part; courage is your part. With those two keys you and I can live, regardless of the circumstances.

On May 21, 1927, while Col. Charles A. Lindbergh was winging his way across the Atlantic Ocean, an editorial headed LINDBERGH FLIES ALONE was printed in the *New York Sun*:

Alone?

Is he alone at whose right side rides Courage, with Skill within the cockpit, Faith upon the left? Does solitude surround the man when Adventure leads the way and Ambition reads the dials?

Alone? With what other companions would that man fly to whom the choice was given?

Fountain of Youth

When Junior heads off to State University and Sally hears wedding bells, that's no reason for closing the family homestead. When there is a *why* to life, growing old does not mean giving up.

In the words of one woman, "I decided we couldn't just rot because the kids are gone. So I fixed a candlelight supper and the works—surprised my husband to death! From here on, good-bye to middle-age doldrums. Hello, Life!"

And from a sixty-year-old grandmother, "My age group still has time to repair outlooks and have a better closing period together. This grandma came to life," she reported. "Instead of just an old lady, I'm a girl at heart and my husband loves it. This elixir of life is guaranteed to turn your life rightside up and stand your man on his ear and keep his head above Cloud Nine. I know because I share it with him."

Age is so relative. I have known some middle-aged women who could pass for twenty years older. But I have known some eighty-four-year-olds (Charlie's grand-mother, Mimi, for example) who go to work daily, scrub their own floors and even travel abroad by themselves.

One such "young at heart" thanked me for "lighting a fire under one lazy wife." She said, "My family wonders where the old grouch went (the old me) and we are so much happier. When my attitude changed, so did my resentment. I do believe I'll be in a rocking chair next to my love when I'm ninety!"

She closed by saying, "The excitement that I thought was gone forever has returned. The future looks bright and the word 'forever' seems like a gift from heaven."

As a naval wife stationed abroad, Sharon felt that the inconveniences were almost impossible to bear until she found hope and courage. "I decided to stop drowning myself in pity," she said, "and start loving the few nights when he is home and take each 'duty day' with a smile. Now I get sheer pleasure out of catering to Gene's every need, including all the extras which some women con-sider 'weren't in the contract,' such as friendship, kind-ness, and togetherness."

Sharon told about their difficult living conditions. Each week the coal man walks through her nicely waxed floors and dumps one hundred pounds of coal in her bathroom linen closet, their only storage room. She starts the fires and cleans up afterwards.

She said, "It's difficult to turn a 'cinder witch' into a sexy Cinderella with coal dust under my once-perfectly manicured fingernails in a house so cold you can see fog from your breath. When a down draft comes from the fireplace, smoke, soot, and an unhealthy, almost-unbearable film covers the entire room."

The 4:30 bubble bath is out of the question for her because of the cold. Electricity is too expensive to use. Irons and mixers are out, since they require a transformer. There is no such thing as a shopping center, just plenty of bakeries—"woman's worst enemy."

"I could go on and on," she said, "but this gives you an idea of the things I am doing willingly now for my husband. I hope I can share my experiences with others so that their lives too might become more meaningful. P.S. I am only nineteen."

Why to Live

After serving five grueling years in a North Viet Nam prison, Captain James H. Warner shared the secret of his survival. As a POW he had been locked in a six-by-six-foot "hot-box" and not allowed to sleep for ten days. He was shackled and forced to sit on a twelve-inch-high stool for periods of up to twenty days.

During that confinement he told himself, "You must look life squarely in the eye, and say that regardless of whatever it is, I'm going to do all that I can to make the most of it. If it's a little room made out of stone that is six feet by six feet and blank walls, then I will have to accept that, and I'll have to make the most out of it."

Nietzche said, "He who has a *why* to live can bear almost any *how*." All across the globe, creative and courageous women are living proof that when a woman is filled with His joy, circumstances will not rob her of that joy.

Armed with a *why* to live, a New York housewife said, "I have been married eighteen years, I have three teen-age children, multiple sclerosis, and a boring marriage." She had been attending graduate school, but was unable to finish her master's degree due to her illness.

"I can't work or drive or even walk much," she reported, "but God has been good to me. I only wish your book had arrived fifteen years ago. How much happier our lives could have been, and how different they will be from now on! I say that as I sit here in my black-mesh stockings, red mini-skirt and Charlie Chan T-shirt—more fun! God bless you! My husband and I are both pooped, but so happy and it was so easy!"

The letters keep coming.

"Dear Marabel," Marianne began. "My husband and I had called it quits. I left home and headed for my brother's house, thousands of miles away. I was running away from my husband, the man I love as much as life.

"While changing planes in Dallas, I looked for a book to soothe my loneliness and my broken heart, and there I bought your book. I never put it down. By the time I got to the end of the line, I had read it nonstop, cover to cover. I didn't want to make a new life single, but wanted to go home and make a new life there.

"I called and left a message for my husband, 'I'm on my way home. If he wants to start anew, tell him to please come for me!'

"It was the longest six hours I'd ever spent, not know-

ing if he'd be there. Oh, how I prayed he'd be there
. . . and he was! It cost me $245 to find a $1.95 book—
that saved my marriage and my life."

Lake of Love

A Total Woman keeps her priorities in order. First
she's a *person,* responsible to God. Second, if she's married, she's a *partner.* Third, if she has children, she's a
parent. And finally, her fourth priority is to the *public.*
You, then him, then kids, then others.

Jump feet first into the Lake of Love and the ripples
will flow out in every direction. The ripples from a
changed life reach not only a husband and children, but
the public as well. Allow me to share some more good
news from changed lives.

1. *You.* That's where it all starts. Listen to the personal
joy of these women:

•From California—"I'm sure it won't be all peaches
and cream from now on, but I've got a good start. I feel
so good inside. My life is right side up and the whole
world is beautiful again."

•From Kentucky—"I know already that neither my
husband or I will ever be the same again . . . and am I
happy!"

2. *Him.* A happy marriage can only be created by happy
people.

•From Oregon—"I was a T.W. (Temperamental

Witch) and my marriage was a T.W. (Total Wreck). My husband lived on a powder keg waiting for me to explode. I'm so grateful I changed before we spent the rest of our lives making each other miserable. Now he's delirious with joy!"

•From Ohio—"Our house has become a home again, not just a nice place to visit, but a great place to live. For the first time in years my husband and I are so many things to each other. Most important, good friends!"

•From Wisconsin—"My marriage has gone from rock bottom to the heights in the last six weeks. My husband and children seem so different. Could it be that they have changed or could it be that I have changed? Last night for no reason my husband surprised me with a Neil Diamond album which *he* hates! I feel wonderful again, just like the girl he married."

•From Arizona—"My husband, the cold iceberg whom I had to *beg* to hold me, now can't keep his hands off me, and I love it, I love it, I love it!!!"

•From Nebraska—"Married twenty-one years, I felt my husband never noticed me. It was as if I didn't exist. For three weeks I applied these principles and he's become so nice. He's complimenting *me!* I hope to hear 'I love you' in 1976."

And the ripples keep widening.

3. *Kids.* The kids are usually the first to "catch" the change.

•From Indiana—"Being an introvert, I have always found it difficult to kiss my husband, but last night it seemed so natural. My four-year-old was so amazed he hollered to the other children, 'Come here and look at Mommy and Daddy! I think they are gonna get married!' "

•From Texas—"My little boy said last night, 'Mommy, tomorrow when I get up, you get all my kisses all day.' I feel hope welling up inside, and for the first time I see my home being repaired. Pray for me—I must run to catch up. My husband and I are separated."

•From New York—"Mommy, your eyebrows aren't down anymore. You don't yell anymore."

4. *Them.* "Them" can be anyone and everyone and usually is.

•From Oklahoma—"As a divorcee of six months, I laughed at your book but tried being a Total Woman with my date. Our relationship is now just super. It's getting out of hand though here at work. I manage a men's shoe department and I smile and listen to them instead of sulk. I'm getting many new customers who come in asking for me, and I'm having enormous increases in sales. This is a dangerous book for single women!"

•From South Carolina—"Unfortunately, I must wait for my husband to return from a naval voyage. What a boost to a ship's morale, if we sailors' wives gave them a good send-off. Happy wives mean a happy crew. A happy crew means a good crew. A good crew means a successful voyage. And a successful voyage means an earlier return. Why, we wives owe it to the government to take the Total Woman course!"

•From Washington—"Not having a husband, I give love to my friends, relatives, my two cats, and believe me, it brings big returns. By love I don't imply sex, just loving gestures and voice. P.S. Typed by blind, not edited. I hope your book comes out for the talking-book records or cassettes for the blind."

The Great Race

On Memorial Day last year, Charlie and I watched the Indianapolis 500 race. Seeing those long, sleek cars roaring off at 190 miles an hour, almost touching wheels on both sides, was terribly exciting. (It reminded me of driving our Miami freeways!)

Ten minutes after the race began, the line of cars began to stretch out and the constant circling of the track became monotonous.

Then the scene changed. The network had filmed some footage from inside a car, as it tore around the track showing the race from the driver's perspective.

Now I sat transfixed, forgetting I was in my own living room. As the car rapidly gained speed and began to move fast, faster, *faster* than I had ever experienced before, I hung on for dear life. "We" moved high up on the banked turns and then swerved in and out to pass other cars. My eyes were glued on the road directly ahead. I couldn't even watch the objects flying by, afraid that "we" might crack up if I didn't concentrate.

What an example of life! So many people think they're in the driver's seat, and they're not even in the car. They would much rather watch from the sidelines and criticize the drivers, than actually get out on the road.

The fun is in the doing. Maybe it's easier to watch, but it's a lot more fun to do, and the most fun to finish!

Success does not depend upon winning the race. Success is entering the race and finishing, knowing you have done your job well.

As we travel on this road of great adventure together, dear friend, you and I both know that life here is difficult. It's a struggle all the way—a glorious struggle at times— a challenge always. Tomorrow, the bottom may fall out and all our efforts may seemingly go down the drain. Nevertheless, we can live in this life above the ruts, walking in the light, clicking our heels for joy.

As one woman told me, "What can I say? At last I know who I am and where I'm going. My children no longer flinch when I hug and kiss them. My husband is thrilled and exhausted with sex. I feel like my life has a new beginning."

Yesterday is gone, today is here, an unused twenty-four-hour slot of time. Regardless of the past, you and I have a new beginning. Today, right now. Not merely an existence, but the possibility of a life of no regrets. Not perfection, but a new perspective. No guarantee of perpetual happiness, but total joy.

I am starting again today right along with you. I'll meet you at the finish line! In the words of the race announcer:

"Ladies, start your engines!"

Bibliography

Butt, Howard. *The Velvet Covered Brick*. New York: Harper & Row, Publishers, 1974.

Dobson, Dr. James. *Hide or Seek*. Old Tappan, N.J.: Fleming H. Revell Co., 1974.

Frankl, Viktor E. *Man's Search for Meaning*. Boston: Beacon Press, rev.ed., 1963.

Fromm, Erich. *The Art of Loving*. New York: Harper & Row, Publishers, 1974.

LaHaye, Tim. *How to Win Over Depression*. Grand Rapids: The Zondervan Corporation, 1974.

Lewis, C.S. *Mere Christianity*. New York: Macmillan, Inc., 1964.

Morgan, Marabel. *The Total Woman*. Old Tappan, N.J.:Fleming H. Revell Co., 1973.

Narramore, Dr. Clyde M. *How to Handle Pressure*. Wheaton, Illinois: Tyndale House Publishers, Inc., 1975.

Scripture References

1 Proverbs 23:7 KJV
2 *See* Genesis 1:26.
3 Proverbs 31:25
4 *See* Matthew 6:25.
5 Proverbs 29:18 KJV
6 Psalms 90:10,12
7 The Amplified Bible puts it, "The reverent and worshipful fear of the Lord prolongs one's days."
8 Proverbs 17:22 KJV
9 Psalms 118:24 KJV
10 *See* Proverbs 27:15.
11 *See* Proverbs 25:24.
12 *See* Mark 3:25 KJV.
13 *See* Ephesians 5:22.
14 *See* Ephesians 5:22 in The Amplified Bible.

15 *See* Matthew 5:38–48.
16 Philippians 4:8
17 Ephesians 4:26,32
18 Proverbs 19:11
19 *See* Proverbs 17:9 KJV.
20 1 Corinthians 13:7
21 Ecclesiastes 6:6
22 *See* Jeremiah 29:13.
23 John 15:11 KJV (*italics* mine)
24 John 8:36 KJV
25 *See* John 10:10.
26 *See* John 15:7;16:24.
27 *See* Psalms 16:11 KJV.
28 Philippians 4:11 KJV
29 2 Timothy 1:7 KJV